The Uncomfortable ' the Macedonian F──── Organization

Victor Sinadinoski

1

Printed in the United States of America

ISBN: 9781728827803

INTRODUCTION

The Macedonian Political Organization (MPO) (presently known as the Macedonian Patriotic Organization) is perhaps one of the most controversial Macedonian Diaspora organizations. On one hand, its official stance has always been the realization of a 'Macedonia for the Macedonians'; its members and followers promote the Macedonian culture; and they call themselves Macedonians. On the other hand, the MPO leadership has often negated the existence of ethnic Macedonians and a Macedonian language, and the MPO bylaws claim that the term 'Macedonian' has no ethnic connotation. Moreover, the bylaws list ethnic groups that hail from Macedonia, which conspicuously does not include ethnic Macedonians.[1] To the MPO leadership and many of its members, the ethnic Macedonian identity is an invention of Yugoslav Communist leader Josip Broz Tito. Yes, the MPO indeed says it is an organization of Macedonians. By this, however, it only means that its members originate from geographical Macedonia and that their language and ethnic identity is Bulgarian. Thus, while on certain levels the MPO can be considered a 'pro-Macedonia' organization, it cannot be classified as a 'pro-Macedonian' group.[2]

Some readers may therefore rightfully find it puzzling that I have expended much effort in writing a book about the MPO. Admittedly, I had hesitations as well, especially because there are ethnic Macedonians and other Macedonian groups more deserving of our understanding and attention. However, I proffer the following reasons to at least clarify my motives for exploring the MPO in depth.

3

First, most regular MPO members and function attendees knew little or nothing about its leadership's ties to fascist Bulgaria. They were repeatedly informed that the MPO was working for Macedonia's independence and against other forces (such as Communists and the Serbian and Greek governments) that sought to keep Macedonia divided. Members of all MPO chapters prior to World War II detested Macedonia's division under Bulgaria, Greece and Serbia. If they had any sympathy for Bulgaria, it was two-fold: one, MPO leaders convinced many followers that the IMRO movement in Pirin Macedonia (Bulgarian Macedonia) was the direct descendent of the IMRO movement that originated in 1893 and that this IMRO was supported by Bulgaria in its endeavors; and two, Pirin Macedonia was essentially a separate state within Bulgaria. Throughout the 1920s and 1930s, IMRO governed, taxed, policed and controlled Pirin Macedonia and it was only formally a political unit of Bulgaria. Therefore, many Macedonians did not feel as threatened by Bulgaria during this period in the same way that they felt threatened by Serbia and Greece. Moreover, as demonstrated by the evidence, many MPO members prior to World War II never identified as Bulgarians. Like many Macedonians, they would sometimes classify their language as Bulgarian if pressed, but this was because Macedonian had not yet been codified. Still, many insisted that they spoke the Macedonian language.

Second, in the late 1940s, the United States branded the Macedonian-American People's League (also known as the Macedonian People's League, a progressive Macedonian group that advocated for the codification of the Macedonian language and recognition of the Macedonian ethnic identity, as well as the establishment of an independent and united Macedonia) as a subversive communist organization and it disintegrated. The MPO then portrayed itself, and was perceived by outsiders, as the only remaining national Macedonian organization in the U.S. From the early 1950s until the Republic of Macedonia's independence in 1991, the MPO was indeed the only visible national organization of Macedonians and it controlled the narrative of the Macedonians' plight. This was the reality despite the obvious fact that most ethnic Macedonians wanted nothing to do with the MPO during this period.

Third, the MPO holds a place in the overall story of the Macedonians' national, ethnic and cultural development abroad, in both negative and positive respects. On the negative side, the MPO refused to associate with the Macedonian ethnic identity, the Macedonian language, and the Macedonian Orthodox Church, even after all three of those became viable realities in the middle of the 20th century. While many Macedonians shook off their pro-Serbian, pro-Bulgarian or pro-Greek biases to join the Macedonian Orthodox Church and identify as Macedonians who spoke the Macedonian language, the MPO core dug its heels in its pro-Bulgarian attitudes. This sowed divisions within the Macedonian-American community. On the positive side, the MPO remained consistent in continuingly promoting the idea of a united and independent Macedonia while providing Macedonian-Americans with many cultural and social opportunities. For those Macedonians who were unaware of the MPO's Bulgarian leanings or who did not have access to other Macedonian groups, this helped preserve many families' Macedonian culture and heritage for several generations.

Moreover, this book is not a comprehensive history of the MPO. For example, it leaves out much of MPO's cultural and social activities and instead examines how the MPO walked the line between being 'pro-Bulgarian' and 'pro-Macedonia'. The MPO is an organization that had many chapters and members who embraced a variety of ideas and viewpoints on the Macedonian identity and people. Additionally, many people who were once MPO members eventually left the group and joined other Macedonian clubs, societies, and church communities that harbored and promoted an ethnic Macedonian identity. Examining and exposing the real story behind the MPO provides Macedonians and scholars with a better understanding of the precise role MPO played (and plays) in the overall story of Macedonian-Americans and the Macedonian Cause.

While for some Macedonians these reasons still do not justify spending time outlining the history of the MPO, I acknowledge that the story of Macedonian-Americans cannot be wholly told without some insight into, and explanation of, the MPO. Just as the story of modern Macedonia cannot be completely told without, for example, insights into Ivan Mihajlov, the right-wing pro-Bulgarian Macedonian gangster, or Ljubco Georgievski, the former Macedonian prime minister who openly embraced a pro-Bulgarian agenda after his tenure expired, the story of Macedonia and Macedonians in America is incomplete without some rendering of MPO's history.

The MPO is a remnant of battles between pro-Serbian, pro-Bulgarian, pro-Greek, and pro-Macedonian forces in Macedonia during the early 20th century, when Bulgaria, Serbia and Greece were circulating propaganda in Macedonia through their respective churches, schools and armed bands. MPO loyalists in the U.S. continued to maintain their pro-Bulgarian position while the pro-Macedonian elements were embracing victory both in the Balkans and in the U.S. While many MPO members were expressing their Macedonian culture and identity, the MPO leadership was constantly under the sway of Bulgarian propaganda, which is rooted in the Bulgarian Government's and Bulgarian Orthodox Church's efforts beginning in the 1870s. This propaganda permeated the minds and hearts of Macedonians for several generations and is not easily uprooted. This has been the sad and unfortunate destiny of the Macedonian nation for many decades.

Taking into consideration that this book examines the MPO in the context of the Macedonian Cause, especially how it relates to Macedonian identity and the creation of a free and independent Macedonia, this book divides the history of the MPO into the following three periods:

A. *The Formative Years, 1921-1944.* This period constitutes the formation of the MPO in the early 1920s and lasts through World War II. This period is defined by staunch support for Mihajlov's IMRO; the creation of an independent and united Macedonia; and accentuated anti-Serbianization of Macedonia.

B. *The True Face, 1945-1990.* This period starts in the late 1940s and lasts through 1990, just as Yugoslavia was beginning to disintegrate. This period is defined by an explicit shift to pro-Bulgarian sympathies; anti-communism; rejection of 'Macedonianism'; and decreasing membership.

C. *The Modern Era, 1991-2018.* This period extends from the Republic of Macedonia's independence in 1991 until the present time. This period is defined by support for Macedonia's independence; increased collaboration and coordination with both Bulgaria's and Macedonia's governments and politicians; an identity crisis; and a shift away from politics and toward cultural activities.

Under this breakdown, this book will provide a clearer picture of the MPO and its relations to, and impact on, the Macedonian Cause. The goal is to uncover the truth of MPO's ideologies and motivations; reveal the inconsistencies and ambiguities in its membership's loyalties; and to determine its proper place in the larger story of Macedonians in America. It is by no means an endorsement of the MPO; rather, it is an acknowledgment of the role it played in the history of Macedonian-Americans and the Macedonian Cause.

PART I: The Formative Years

ONE
The People Behind MPO

The MPO was officially incorporated as a non-profit organization in Indiana in 1925. Three MPO directors – Theodore Vasiloff, Stanley Georgieff and Gill Shishcoff, all based in Indianapolis – submitted the articles of incorporation on July 6. According to their submission, MPO's purpose was as follows:

For the mutual assistance and protection of people of Macedonian race – and for the liberation of Macedonia from political entities – and to foster the ancient right of Macedonia as a state and nation – all as more fully set out in its bylaws – but nothing to conflict with any law or treaty of the United States of America or the laws of Canada.[3]

For those who are familiar with the perceived history of MPO (both those inside and outside the organization), a couple aspects of this official statement could be deemed startling. First, it refers to "people of Macedonian race". This may be surprising to some because historically, as this book will detail, the MPO leadership has officially denied the existence of a Macedonian ethnicity. According to the views of MPO leaders post-World War II, the MPO has persistently negated the existence of a Macedonian ethnicity. Recently, some former MPO leaders acknowledged the existence of ethnic Macedonians but have refrained from classifying the MPO as an ethnic Macedonian organization.

Thus, it is curious that some MPO leaders had once referred to Macedonians as constituting a separate race. To clarify, the term 'race' during this period was commonly used to refer to groups of people that we generally now refer to as 'ethnicities.' In early 20th century Macedonia, for example, Western authors would describe the struggles of the various 'races', which included Macedonians, Bulgarians, Greeks, Serbians, Vlachs and Albanians. The term 'ethnicity' was not commonly used in this sense until after World War II. Moreover, the term 'nationality' was also a commonly used word in the Balkans during this time and was often used interchangeably with 'race'.

Nevertheless, the term 'race' emphasizes certain physical and genetic traits that distinguish a group of people from other groups of people. That these original MPO directors chose to classify the Macedonians as a separate race speaks volumes to their perceptions of themselves as a people in relation to other peoples, especially in comparison to other Balkan peoples.

Moreover, the directors spoke of Macedonia's right to statehood and nationhood as an 'ancient' one. This likewise may seem contradictory or perplexing for those (again, both those inside and outside of MPO) who have only known MPO to have accepted a Bulgarian history for the Slavic-language speaking inhabitants of Macedonia. In this supposed Bulgarian history, it is alleged that Macedonia only recently broke away from Bulgaria and that, since the time the Bulgars arrived in the Balkans (which was well after the years of Alexander the Great and the Roman occupation), Macedonia and Bulgaria were inseparable entities, one and the same. Thus, an MPO member speaking about Macedonia's ancient rights does not seem to neatly fit with the pro-Bulgarian narrative of what the MPO is known to have regularly dispersed into the world.

However, we should not be as taken aback by this blatant 'pro-Macedonian' stance as some of us likely are. This early MPO expression of Macedonian nationalism should only come as a surprise to those who zealously believe one of the following three things: 1) ethnic Macedonians do not exist (and that anyone who classifies himself as such is really ethnic Bulgarian); 2) ethnic Macedonians evolved from ethnic Bulgarians beginning in the late 1920s and 1930s; and 3) the MPO was only and always a pro-Bulgarian organization. Through many studies and researches, it has been undeniably demonstrated that there was a numerous and consistent attachment to a separate Macedonian identity (in the ethno-national sense) since at least the 1870s.[4] So, why should we be surprised that Macedonians identified themselves as a separate race and as an ancient nation during the 1920s?

The answer lies in the abundance of evidence we have from other MPO members and leaders who, if not pro-Bulgarian to begin with, soon sailed the MPO into pro-Bulgarian seas. The directors listed above – those ones tasked with MPO's incorporation – were not the everlasting face of MPO. Unfortunately, not much is known about the extent of their MPO involvement or immigration to America. We only read again about Theodore Vasiloff in Indiana from a 1958 *Indianapolis Star* article, which detailed how Vasiloff was robbed at gunpoint in his liquor store.[5] There is some more information on Stanley Georgieff: the *Indianapolis Star* listed him as a member of the First Presbyterian Church choir in 1932,[6] and he petitioned for U.S. citizenship in Indianapolis on October 18, 1928[7] and was naturalized on January 25, 1929 at the age of 23.[8] Regarding Gill Shishcoff, it is likely that 'Shishcoff' was a misspelling in the Secretary of State filing. The *Indianapolis News* report on MPO's incorporation lists him as Gill Sarbinoff. Sarbinoff seems to be a more plausible surname, as there was a Gill Sarbinoff listed as the elected Vice President of MPO in 1925.[9] He was born in Aegean Macedonia (northern Greece) in 1888 and immigrated to the U.S. in 1907;[10] he became a naturalized U.S. citizen on September 26, 1930 in Indianapolis;[11] and he died in August of 1933.[12]

There is not much more known about these men and their involvement in the MPO or in Macedonian affairs generally. Nonetheless, it seems that their statement of MPO's purpose (regardless of if it was penned by them or not) did not resonate with the known leanings and beliefs of many MPO leaders during that time. To better understand MPO's views on Macedonia and the Macedonian identity, and subsequently MPO's identity, we must better understand MPO's founders, its formation, and its evolution during these formative years.

MPO's formation coincided with the revival of the Internal Macedonian Revolutionary Organization (IMRO) after the end of World War I. This new IMRO was not the same as the IMRO that originated in 1893. That IMRO was a revolutionary government as well as a rebellion force that promoted Macedonian nationalism and advocated for workers' (peasants and farmers) rights. This new IMRO not only implemented new methods in achieving its aims, it also formed stronger allegiances with Bulgaria's fascist government and moved away from the trend toward Macedonian nationalism and complete separation from the deep-seated process of Bulgarianization, Serbianization and Hellenization of the Macedonian people. Many former IMRO leaders refused to join this new IMRO; or if they had joined, they either left it voluntarily or were assassinated for opposing IMRO's new direction. Regardless, it retained the IMRO name and was recognized as such by outsiders. Its new leaders were Petar Chaulev, Aleksandar Protogerov and Todor Aleksandrov; but Aleksandrov was soon recognized as the dominant and accepted *de facto* leader of the organization.

In the years after the League of Nations was established in 1919, Aleksandrov sent two trusted loyalists, Jordan Chkatroff and Srebren Poppetrov, to New York City in order "to advocate on behalf of the Macedonian independence movement." The two men discovered that many Macedonian groups and societies existed in the U.S. and Canada, but there was no overarching structure or organizational body to oversee coordination between them.[13] The two IMRO envoys thus set out to organize these Macedonian communities into a pro-IMRO diaspora force.

These two were optimal choices to expand IMRO's reach. Born in Prilep in 1898,[14] Chkatroff eventually became an IMRO loyalist, as well as a member of the Sofia-based Macedonian student society known as 'Vardar' and the Macedonian National Committee in Bulgaria.[15] Poppetrov was born in a village outside of Lerin (Aegean Macedonia) in 1870 and became a leading local IMRO member in the 1890s. Like Chkatroff, he served on the Macedonian National Committee and he also helped organize Macedonian immigrant societies in Bulgaria.[16] Both these men originated from Macedonian regions that witnessed substantial migration to North America, a detail that carried much weight in Macedonian communities throughout the Diaspora, which were each generally comprised of people from only one region, town or village.[17]

15

Before their arrival, however, the fundamentals for creating a large and effective national organization did indeed exist, even though there was a lack of initiative to link them or seriously politicize them. In November of 1921, three important Macedonian groups were established in the U.S.: 'Prilep' in Steelton, Pennsylvania; 'Kostur' in Fort Wayne, Indiana; and 'Prilep' (eventually renamed 'Todor Aleksandrov') in Youngstown, Ohio.[18] Several more groups formed the next year, such as 'Pirin' in Dayton, Ohio; 'Independence' in Duquesne, Pennsylvania; 'Lerin' in Indianapolis, Indiana; 'Fatherland' in Detroit, Michigan; 'Balkanski Kraj' in Lansing, Michigan; and 'Ilinden' in New York City.[19]

These different groups engaged in a variety of social, cultural and political activities. For example, the Macedonian Brotherhood of Prilep in Steelton, as it officially called itself, hosted cultural events and Macedonian dances, such as a fundraising program it presented in January of 1922.[20] Also, in July of that year, the president of the group, J. Stancoff, sent a cable to the League of Nations and the Balkan Committee in London, where he wrote about a divided Macedonia under "three masters" and that their Steelton group consisted of Bulgarians, Romanians and Turks from Macedonia. In its entirety, it read:

Bulgarians, Rumanians and Turks from Macedonia organized in Macedonian Brotherhood Prilep in Steelton, PA., U.S.A., with your permission, beg to submit to your consideration, when you are discussing the rights of minorities, not to forget the unhappy Macedonia, from which three hundred thousand refugees in Bulgaria and thirty thousand in America eagerly await, ever since signing of the peace treaties, to return to their homes under protection of the clause of Rights of Minorities, which clause was never

16

applied in our fatherland divided among three masters unwelcomed by Macedonian people, whose sole desire is Macedonia for Macedonians.[21]

Steelton's Macedonians would soon be divided between pro-Bulgarian MPO Macedonians and those who desired recognition of an ethnic Macedonian identity, language, church and nation. The rift would eventually accumulate to horrific violence.[22]

These Macedonian groups, however, were not representative of the entire Macedonian population. When Detroit's 'Fatherland' group formed in May of 1922, only one-fifth of the initial meeting's 250 attendees decided to become members.[23] While from an organizational standpoint this may have been a welcomed success, because a new group can make significant strides with just 50 members, it is striking that so many Macedonians attended and only so few decided to join. Perhaps 'Fatherland's' domestic and Balkan agenda turned off many Macedonians.

The elected leaders of 'Fatherland' included Simon Balkoff, Atanas Filipoff, Lazar Kocheff, Andrey Kostoff, Lambro Nikoloff, Tom Panas, and Hristo Spiroff.[24] None of these leaders seemed to have had a lasting role or involvement in the MPO movement, as records of their activities and presence is sparse. Balkoff and Filipoff immigrated to Detroit in 1914 and roomed together in the 1920s;[25] Kostoff was around 40 years old when 'Fatherland' formed and was last recorded in the 1930 U.S. Census;[26] Nikoloff first arrived in the U.S. in 1907 and headed to Granite City, Illinois,[27] but soon made his way to Detroit in 1909 at the age of 25;[28] Spiroff was a Detroit resident for several decades (at least through the 1940s);[29] and there is no other readily available information on the rest. As with the 1925 MPO directors who filed MPO's articles of incorporation, these initial Detroit leaders seemed to have faded away from the MPO relevance.

Still, there were several thriving Macedonian communities scattered throughout North America, especially in the Midwest and greater-Toronto area, which provided fertile organizing ground for IMRO's agents in America. This fact is corroborated by Poppetrov's statements in a 1924 letter, where he mentions that he visited 33 cities with sizeable communities of Macedonians that could benefit from the formation of societies or organizations, but that there was "no initiative or urge to do so." He further wrote:

I went to America (the United States and Canada), I traveled all the cities where there were large sums of displaced Bulgarians and I returned to Bulgaria.

The Bulgarians in America are in large majority from Macedonia. Before the wars, these Macedonian-Bulgarians went, earned money, and returned to their native country. After the wars, not only do they not return to their loved ones, but they almost always call for their families to come here. ...

The universe does not lose the fact that some of them are not called Orthodox, but instead Protestants or Catholics, and that some have lost a national Bulgarian feeling and are called Serbs, Greeks, Russians or whatever ... If our nation is organized faithfully and nationally, it will only be saved for the future reintegration of our homeland of Macedonia and for the kingdom, but by then it will be a force that will be taken into account in solving our big questions. ...

All these collections of nationalities and associations co-organized by nationality, faith, economy, charity, church-

school and politics have their churches, schools, clubs, flags, trustees and governing bodies, convene assemblies and congregations, issue national newspapers, celebrate solemnly all their national holidays, make anniversaries of people deserving in their native places, do demonstrations and manifestations of their own people's questions, and live distinct and recognized national lives in Great and Free America. Only the Bulgarians have remained behind in the above-mentioned acquisitions there unorganized.[30]

Poppetrov recognized a need to organize these Macedonians. Thus, he took a leading effort in planning and organizing the first national convention of these scattered Macedonian societies and groups that would eventually become the MPO.[31]

This first convention convened in Fort Wayne on October 1, 1922 and lasted several days. In addition to Fort Wayne's Macedonians, other Macedonian groups from Michigan, New York, Pennsylvania, Ohio and Indiana sent members to represent their respective organizations, while two Macedonian groups in Ohio sent telegrams of support.[32]

Atanas Stefanoff of Fort Wayne called the meeting to order and "outlined the tragic condition of the newly-enslaved Macedonia." He then urged the Macedonians to combine their groups' efforts into a "strong and patriotic Macedonian organization."[33] The delegates present enthusiastically "supported the idea of creating a free independent and united Macedonia."[34] Moreover, many of the delegates favored naming their organization the Macedonian Patriotic Organization (which it eventually became in the 1950s); however, some savvy political thinkers rejected the term 'patriotic' because that term "had assumed a repulsive meaning" after the Central Powers lost the First World War.[35] Others wanted to call it the Macedonian Brotherhood, but that name was rejected because "it coincided with the names of the organized [Macedonian] groups in Bulgaria."[36] The delegates found the term 'political' to be most appropriate and they thus branded themselves as the Macedonian Political Organization.

The elected chairman and vice-chairman for this convention were Mihail Nikoloff and Kosta Popoff, respectively. The delegates eventually elected Atanas Stefanoff as president; Trayan Nikoloff, vice-president; Mihail Nikoloff, Interim Secretary; Atanas Lebamoff, Treasurer; and Pavel Angeloff, Advisor. Lazar Kisselincheff was tasked with the duty of drafting MPO's bylaws.[37]

Some of these men would proceed to play critical roles in these early years, so it is useful to understand them better. Kosta Popoff, who would eventually serve as MPO's vice-president and then president, was born in Vladovo (near Voden, Aegean Macedonia). After the Second Balkan War concluded in 1913 and Greece was in control of Aegean Macedonia, he fled to the U.S. and settled in Pennsylvania. He eagerly participated in MPO's foundation, insisting that while "close contact with the Macedonian Brotherhoods in Bulgaria" was necessary, the MPO should be "a completely independent entity pursuing the same goal – a free and independent Macedonia."[38]

Atanas Lebamoff was born in Visheni and was active in the MPO until his death in 1932. Perhaps he is not remembered as much for his role as treasurer in the organization but for the MPO contributions of those sharing a close bloodline with him. His daughter Dita was actively involved in MPO and eventually married Peter Atzeff, who also held several high-ranking positions in the MPO. Lebamoff's brother,

20

Argir, who was 11 years his younger and also active in the MPO, was the father of Ivan and George Lebamoff, who themselves would serve on the MPO Central Committee.[39] Argir's grandson, Jordan, is MPO's current president.[40]

Lazar Kisselincheff played an integral role in the first years of MPO's existence. His past was more intriguing than his MPO role, however. Born in the 1870s, he was an IMRO loyalist for many years, with close ties to IMRO giants Gjorche Petrov[41] and Goce Delchev, as evidenced by a letter Kisselincheff wrote to Delchev after the former was arrested in Greece for suspected arms trafficking.[42] He helped to establish the Macedonian National Committee in Athens, where he was educated since childhood, and was well-known for smuggling weapons from Greece and Albania into Macedonia before the 1903 Macedonian Ilinden (St. Elijah's Day) Uprising.[43] He first moved to the U.S. in 1911 and would often travel back and forth between the U.S. and the Balkans. Kisselincheff was integral to helping Poppetrov organize the North American Macedonian groups in fraternities like those of the Macedonian brotherhoods in Bulgaria.[44]

These were certainly not the only men who played critical roles in these formative years. Christo Nizamoff, who was born in Resen during the middle of the Ilinden Uprising, came to the U.S. in 1921. In 1922, he read an article in the *Naroden Glas* (People's Voice), a Macedonian paper published in Granite City, Illinois, that called for the Macedonian organizations in U.S. to unite. Nizamoff responded to the article by publishing an article in the paper that caught the attention of Kisselincheff. Kisselincheff immediately wrote to Nizamoff asking to meet him in New York City and to consider being involved in the establishment of a national Macedonian organization, which was to take place in Fort Wayne in October of 1922.[45]

In New York, Kisselincheff told Nizamoff that the Fort Wayne conference would task them "for the time being... [with] refuting the Serbian and Greek propaganda trying to justify their oppressive regime in Macedonia."[46] Shortly after, Nizamoff attended the New York 'Ilinden' group's meeting, where he met Nicholas Stoyanoff, president of the organization. Nicholas, who was married to an Irish-American woman who had been involved in the Irish independence movement, suggested that Nizamoff be the secretary of their local group.[47] Although Nizamoff did not attend the Fort Wayne Convention in October, he was eventually appointed Director of the Macedonian Press Bureau in New York to promote the 'Macedono-Bulgarian' point of view.[48] It was not long, however, before Nizamoff was called to work for the Macedonian Cause out of MPO's central office in Indiana.

It was in 1924, in Indiana, where the momentum for MPO accelerated. The convention (held again in Fort Wayne) saw Jordan Chkatroff as the main guest. Todor Aleksandrov, IMRO's leader, had personally sent him to the U.S. to fortify MPO's work and turn it into a serious organization. He was instrumental in bringing over several important Macedonians from the Macedonian Student Organization 'Vardar' in Sofia, such as Boris Zografoff, Assen Avramoff, Petar Atzeff, and Luben Dimitroff. Accordingly, Chkatroff was elected secretary at the convention, and Pandel Shaneff and Tashe Popcheff were elected president and secretary, respectively, and were in those roles for nearly two decades.[49]

At the 1926 convention, held in Harrisburg, it was finally decided that the time was ripe to begin publishing a weekly newspaper. The MPO Central Committee had desired such a newspaper from MPO's inception, but they had neither the membership nor money to successfully execute such a task. Now, however, the timing was ideal. The purpose of the paper "would be to spread and defend the idea of a free and independent state of Macedonia[,] stress the historic fact that the majority of the Macedonian people were of Bulgarian origin...and justify the existence of revolutionary organizations working against the oppressive regime of the Belgrade and Athens governments."[50]

The MPO decided the paper would be called the *Macedonian Tribune*. The Central Committee (then led by Shaneff) originally wanted Krsto Velvanov, a respected intellectual in Sofia, to be the paper's editor. However, Velvanov refused the responsibility due to ill health and instead recommended Boris Zografoff. Zografoff was originally from Bitola and was working for the Publishing House of Bulgaria's Foreign Ministry at the time. Velvanov clamored about Zografoff: "He is experienced, knows French fluently and is a talented journalist and writer. He is also a dedicated and devoted champion of our cause."[51] The Central Committee enthusiastically welcomed Velvanov's recommendation and Chkatroff ensured Zografoff made it to the U.S.

Nizamoff and Kisselincheff met with Zografoff when he arrived in New York City in January of 1927. He did not know any English, but the two men helped him navigate his duties and MPO's expectations. After three days of meetings with Nizamoff and Kisselincheff, Zografoff boarded a train for Indianapolis, the established central headquarters of MPO. A month later, the first issue of the *Macedonian Tribune* was published.[52]

The next few years, however, brought some significant divisions and turmoil within MPO. These divisions were triggered by events unfolding in the Balkans and tested the loyalties and allegiances of MPO's members. To understand these divisions, a brief outline of the events unfolding in Macedonia at the time is helpful.

After the end of World War I and the restructuring of IMRO, the Macedonians had split into several factions (which had actually begun two decades earlier). One faction aligned with the Communists and another considered themselves Federalists. These two factions shared many similar views, such as an autonomous and united Macedonia in a potential Balkan Federation and recognition of the Macedonian nation (and eventually language); however, they had some minor political differences that prevented prolonged and steady collaboration.

Another group, dominated by Todor Aleksandrov and Aleksandar Protogerov, supported an independent Macedonia but had closer ties with the Bulgarian government and right-wing elements throughout Bulgaria. They were thus ideologically and strategically opposed to the Federalist and Communist Macedonians. Moreover, the Communists and Federalists advocated more peaceful and legal methods for their aims while Aleksandrov's faction believed in an uptick in violent revolutionary methods.

Still, in 1924, Aleksandrov joined with the Communists and Federalists in declaring a common approach to solving the Macedonian Question. The story gets murky here, but a few weeks after Aleksandrov sent Chkatroff to the U.S.,

Aleksandrov was murdered. Some say he was murdered by left-wing Macedonians for publicly denying his collaboration with the Communists; and some say Protogerov was behind the murder. A more commonly accepted theory is that Ivan Mihajlov, one of Aleksandrov's close associates that had gained the trust of Bulgaria's fascist and right-wing leaders, had ordered the murder at the Bulgarian government's behest. The Bulgarian government and Mihajlov would not tolerate Aleksandrov making deals with the Communists, which would impede Bulgaria's quest to keep its part of Macedonia under its realm and to eventually see Macedonia's unification under a Great Bulgaria. Mihajlov was asked to order Aleksandrov in exchange for guaranteed protection as IMRO's new leader.

Soon, Mihajlov was considered the 'king' of Pirin Macedonia and he began administering this kingdom ruthlessly. His unforgiving gangster-like approach to running Macedonia boiled over when, in 1928, Mihajlov ordered the murder of Protogerov, supposedly as punishment for Protogerov's alleged involvement in Aleksandrov's murder. This divided IMRO into two factions: Mihajlovists and Protogerovists. (There was also a third branch called IMRO-United, left-wing Macedonians who were staunchly anti-Bulgarian.) This split in IMRO resulted in much bloodshed, with hundreds, if not thousands, of murders and assassinations taking place over several years as the factions fought for domination.[53]

These developments profoundly impacted MPO's members, especially its leadership. Zografoff, the *Tribune* editor, feverishly stood against Mihajlovists and their violent methods. Assen Avramoff, who was born in Sofia but whose family hailed from the Drama region in Aegean Macedonia, arrived in the U.S. on September 25, 1929.[54] A graduate of Sofia's Law School, he was elected as secretary to the MPO Central Committee in order to replace Jordan Chkatroff, who had left for the Balkans 1929 to act as "prime minister" of Mihajlov's IMRO, as well as loyal adviser to Ivan Mihajlov.[55] Avramoff was staunchly pro-Mihajlov. He was described as a good friend and confidant of Mihajlov.[56] Nizamoff had noted that, since Avramoff's arrival, Zografoff and Avramoff "were not on speaking terms."[57]

Even though Zografoff was against Mihajlov's methods, he believed that the MPO should not choose sides in the internal struggles overseas.[58] Furthermore, unlike several of his MPO associates, he maintained that just because Macedonians' language was classified as 'Bulgarian', it did not mean Macedonia and Macedonians should not be independent or considered as their own people. In 1929, he wrote:

The Serbians have closed all of the non-Serbian churches, schools and libraries; have expelled, imprisoned, tortured or killed bishops, preachers, teachers in Macedonia; have placed in prison and tortured Macedonian and Croatian students; have arrested, imprisoned, tortured, expelled or killed many Macedonian, Montenegrin and Croatian patriots, business men, educators, for the simple reason of their unwillingness to change their nationality. ...

Mr. Vukovich "calls Macedonia a myth." Macedonia existed even before Serbia. Macedonia has fought Turkey and is fighting the new oppressors, Servia and Greece, to become free and independent. In this struggle for freedom lives have been lost on all sides. The peace of the world has been threatened. Is that a myth? Now there is a revolution in Macedonia against Servia and Greece. Is that a myth?

Mr. Vukovich states since there is no Macedonian language, Macedonia should not be independent. If that argument holds good Switzerland, Austria [and] even the United States should not be independent. The language does not govern the making of a country. When the population of a given territory of a considerable size wants to be free and independent, as the original American colonies wanted to be free and independent, this population has right to establish an independent country. This is the principle of the American Declaration of independence.[59]

Zografoff's views and writings were much more blatantly pro-Macedonian – and much less Bulgarian-friendly – than those of most other early MPO leaders, as we will see in Chapter Two. In opposition to Zografoff, Avramoff and other MPO leaders wanted to align with Mihajlov.[60] These members considered Mihajlov to be Macedonia's number one "warrior".[61] These differences accumulated and climaxed at MPO's 1930 convention. Nizamoff described the mood of that convention:

The Youngstown convention was stormy. Tempers ran high. I had been elected chairman and there were moments when I, too, lost my temper. The divisions and battles of the IMRO across the ocean had affected all of us. During the first and second days the sessions continued until early midnight. But the time came when all of us had to think for the preservation of our organization. Finally, with some help from me, Avramoff, presenting his case with the mastery and logic of a jurist, succeeded in swaying most of the delegates to his viewpoint and the neutrality voted the year before was rescinded. The MPO in the United States agreed to support the side which had punished-General Protogeroff "to save the Macedonian movement from a takeover by incompetent and corrupt left-wingers".[62]

These "left-wingers" would go on to be the advocates of a free and autonomous Macedonia, as well as for recognition of the Macedonian ethnicity and language. Many of the left-wingers in MPO would eventually leave and join the Macedonian People's League, MPL, and give MPO further troubles.

Still, the 1930 Youngstown Convention highlighted real divisions. Zografoff resigned as *Tribune* editor. Nizamoff describes MPO President Shaneff's dilemma, as well:

Mr. Shaneff was a close friend of Zografoff, and he too considered stepping aside. Taking into consideration the prevailing atmosphere and the uncompromising attitude of some of the delegates, Mr. Shaneff's pending resignation would have created a divisive split in the organization. Some of the most influential and concerned delegates then gathered together and contacted Mr. Shaneff. They presented their case to him. He listened patiently and politely and finally said: "My friends, I do not want to see a split in the MPO any more than you do. We are going to accept."[63]

As a viable organization, the MPO was saved. However, the Macedonian Cause in the North America remained fractured and would continue to remain fractured for several decades. Soon after this convention, Zografoff published an article warning of the impending doom lurking over Europe because of narrow nationalism, which could only be described as a reaction to the events that unfolded three weeks earlier at the MPO convention. His 1930 editorial read, in part:

More than ten years has passed since the war. Many events have occurred in this period and they showed that the world war, especially the peace treaties, did not bring the expected peace, security and justice in the world. We are witnesses of

a reviving, and perhaps strong, spirit of narrow nationalism, as a militant force, opposed to some nationalism of other people, which spirit is dividing Europe into new hostile camps.

Great efforts are to be made to save humanity from a new war, which might destroy the whole world. In my opinion, the elementary duty in the present time of every citizen in every country is: To preach and to work for the rooting in the heart's feelings of brotherhood not only toward people of former allied countries, but also toward people of every nation, and for the rooting in the conscience of the generation that the only way to attain peace and security in the international life is the way of justice and good will among all nations of the world.[64]

This was Zografoff's final public word on the matter. In his wisdom, he saw the need for not only the Macedonians to unite against fascism and narrow nationalism, but for the world's countries to do the same. He forewarned of drastic consequences if not – and history proved him right.

With Zografoff gone, the MPO now needed to replace him. At the Youngstown convention, they appointed Luben Dimitroff as editor. Dimitroff – more about him in a moment – was still in Sofia, however, so they sought to fill the void until his arrival in 1931.[65] Avramoff volunteered to edit the *Tribune* for the time being.[66] During his stint as editor, the *Tribune* began publishing hundreds of articles detailing the lives of revolutionaries who died fighting the Serbian government in Vardar Macedonia (Serbian-occupied Macedonia, today the Republic of Macedonia). The *Tribune* furthermore began to expose spies, betrayers and traitors to Mihajlov's IMRO.[67] In this way, MPO was finally doing the propaganda and 'legal' work for Mihajlov's IMRO.

It was not just through publishing Mihajlov's writings, such as when, in 1936, the MPO published a booklet by Ivan Mihajlov (who was writing under the name Balkanicus at the time) justifying IMRO's assassinations of Serbian officials,[68] that MPO was serving Mihajlov's agenda. In 1999, the U.S. Central Intelligence Agency (CIA) released a confidential 1953 document that highlighted the real connection between Ivan Mihajlov's IMRO and the MPO throughout the 1930s and 1940s. In part, the CIA operative stated:

The US branch of the IMRO is the Macedonian Political Organization [MPO] which, through its secretary Luben Dimitroff, acts as a money raising organ to support Ivan Mihailov. Dimitroff is completely subservient to Mihailov who sets the policy for MPO activities in the US. Dimitroff and several of his staff are paid for their work, while Ivan Mihailov receives approximately US $8,000 per year plus expenses. Although the money to pay the salaries is raised in the US very few people know that Ivan Mihailov is hiding in Italy under an assumed name which unfortunately, I do not know.[69]

Not only did the MPO begin advocating for Mihajlov's and IMRO's goals and beliefs, they soon became Mihajlov's champions, even when most Macedonians worldwide despised him.

The CIA further detailed that Mihajlov cooperated with the Nazis during World War II. It then insisted that Avramoff had been sent to North America by Mihajlov "to strengthen the MPO, collect more money and also to spot the opposition to the MPO both in Canada and the US." The CIA exposed Mihajlov even further:

In 1945, when Tito created an autonomous Communist Macedonia, the MPO congress in the US sent a congratulatory telegram to Tito...Later, when Tito broke from Moscow, the MPO and Mihailov broke with Tito...Recently, Mihailov sent to the US two of his most trusted associates who are currently in Detroit. They are: Ivan Vassilev who has become president of the MPO branch in Detroit; Vassilev's real name is Ivan Ilchev but he changed it so he could enter the US. The other henchman is Argir Nikolov.[70]

The CIA operative concluded: "I would say that Ivan Mihailov is a gangster, terrorist who cannot be trusted by the US or anyone; he runs the IMRO and the MPO entirely for his own advancement."[71] Even author Joseph Roucek, in his 1948 book *Balkan Politics*, wrote that "the aims of the Macedonian Political Organizations were at first 'to work in a legal manner for the independence of Macedonia'; after 1931, however, and especially after 1933, the influence of Mihailoff prevailed. The organization contributed large sums of money to Mihailoff's cause and tried to appeal to the American public on its behalf."[72]

It is because of this reality, which the CIA and others recognized over seven decades ago (the true nature of Mihajlov, his aims and his methods) that the MPO found itself under constant attacks by the "left-wing" Macedonian groups that were adamantly anti-Mihajlov. For example, in September of 1932, Toronto MPO members got into a melee with Macedonians belonging to the Macedonian Progressive and National Organization (MPNO). MPO members accused the MPNO of being Communists. MPNO countered by "accusing members of [the MPO] of being sympathetic to Bulgaria instead of working for Macedonian independence." In this fight, "chairs, jugs, fists and even a knife were used, sending eight men to hospital for scalp-wound treatment" and "two men suffered abdominal wounds." About 100 people were involved in the fight, and scores of others suffered minor injuries.[73]

Two years later, an anonymous MPO member submitted an editorial to the *Akron Beacon* that, on the surface, appeared to be quite pro-Macedonian:

The strong Macedonian freedom seeking political organization [MPO] of United States and Canada make drastic cuts to free themselves of the 'blood sucking unjust European vampires.' Along with the Macedonian political organizations are the communists and socialists who demand rights, justice and equality...Serbia and Greece divided the famous ancient country, Macedonia. Will they let the Macedonians have their own churches? No! Their own schools? No! What constitutional rights then do these Macedonians have? None whatever![74]

In reply to this, however, another Macedonian responded by condemning the author's views, especially for MPO's Mihajlov ties:

I state that the Macedonian political organizations are neither strong, nor effective in scaring these Fascist governments, and furthermore, the parent organization of the Macedonian political organization in Europe, the so-called 'Interior Macedonian Revolutionary Organization', under the leadership of Evan Mihailoff, is helping the Bulgarian king and his government to kill the Macedonian progressives such as Dimo H. Dimoff, Karakiroff, Hristo Traveoff and many others which were shaving the stability of the Bulgarian Fascist government, and thus creating a misunderstanding in the Macedonian revolutionary movement. Secondly, they never cooperated with the communists, nor socialists, which, from a revolutionary standpoint, are the real friends of the oppressed, and economically exploited people. The real fight against the

governments and its helpers in undertaken by the IMRO-United, in Macedonia itself and the Macedonian People's league of United States and Canada.[75]

Later that year, at the MPO convention, four MPL members were arrested for passing out handbills, without having paid the necessary licensing fees, that criticized Mayor William Hosey and other speakers attending the MPO event. The handbills stated that "city officials did not know the type of person they were greeting," alluding to MPO's fascist Bulgarian ties.[76]

At the closing of the 1935 MPO convention, the MPL circulated a statement denying that the MPO "represents the suffering and heroic struggle of the Macedonian people for national liberty." The circular emphasized that MPO's members were being misled; "that their leaders [were] Macedonian fascist agents of Bulgarian imperialisms and that two of its leaders, Peter Atseff, general secretary, and L. Dimitroff, editor of the Macedonian Tribune, were imported from fascist Bulgaria." It pleaded with the MPO to "throw out of [its] ranks the fascist leaders and murderers of your brothers, friends and sisters and unite with us in a joint struggle against the tyrants of Macedonia." Nizamoff publicly denied these allegations and declared the MPL a communist organization.[77]

There were many more confrontations between the MPO and left-wing Macedonian groups in North America. These attacks would culminate into more stabbings and shootings. However, it is clear that by the end of World War II, the MPO was not simply an organization of 'Macedonia for the Macedonians', but it was instead Mihajlov's propaganda tool that aimed to keep as many Macedonians as possible within Bulgaria's orbit. Bulgaria had dreams of recapturing Macedonian territory, or at least of being in *de facto* control of Macedonia, and Mihajlov's type of Macedonianism (pro-Bulgarian and fascist) was Bulgaria's best bet. Eventually, Bulgaria's government would change power many times, between right-wing and left-wing leaders; but the MPO continued to support and promote Mihajlov's ideals until his death in 1990.

TWO
To Attack Serbia & Greece (Sometimes Bulgaria)

The MPO's mission throughout this period was to provide a relentless barrage of information against the Serbian and Greek governments. When Ivan Mihajlov found himself an enemy of the Bulgarian government, the MPO would occasionally attack Bulgaria, too. But this criticism of Bulgaria was infrequent and not as piercing. While the MPO consistently described Macedonia as divided between Bulgaria, Greece, and Serbia and called for Macedonia's reunification and independence, Serbia and Greece were the ones generally labeled as the oppressors and enslavers.

The MPO utilized its conventions, its publications (such as the *Macedonian Tribune*), and U.S. newspapers to meticulously detail Macedonia's predicament and MPO's goals for Macedonia. Noticeably, there are some variations in opinion between individual members and during different years as MPO's allegiance shifted toward Mihajlov, as we will see.

MPO's nearly century-long vision of Macedonia as a 'Switzerland of the Balkans' has its roots at the 1923 convention, when MPO adviser Pavel Angeloff spoke passionately to the gathered delegates:

The solution of the Macedonian question and the Balkan question will be accomplished through the establishment of an independent and autonomous state which automatically will give all people political and civil rights and liberties

similar to those in all advanced countries. The independence of Macedonia, accompanied by the necessary motives of harmony in the political policy of the Balkans, will call forth the establishment of a Balkan federation similar to the United States or Switzerland.[78]

Angeloff's address was similar to that call of many Macedonians – including Federalists and Communists – that sought to incorporate a united Macedonia into a Balkan Federation. While the call for a Balkan federation would not be as prominent in later MPO statements, it is significant to note that Angeloff called the potential Balkan federation a 'Switzerland'. In the future, MPO would evolve this ideal into Mihajlov's official stance on the Macedonian Question: Macedonia should be a 'Switzerland of the Balkans'. This Macedonia would be similar to Switzerland, where different ethnic groups resided side-by-side, none of which were ethnic Swiss, but all calling themselves Swiss nationals. Macedonia would consist of several ethnic groups – none of them Macedonian – but all of them would be Macedonian nationals. Angeloff's speech seems to indicate, instead, that Macedonians would form one branch of a larger Switzerland called the Balkan Federation. The Macedonians, accordingly, were one of the several Balkan peoples.

This second annual convention also resulted in the MPO passing resolutions that "demanded changes to be made in the treaties of Bucharest, Neuilly and Versailles to turn Macedonia over again to its own people in order to preserve peace in the Balkans." These treaties had cemented Macedonia's division and subjugation amongst her neighbors and were deserving of such criticism. One particular resolution was especially harshly worded and did not pander to the pro-Bulgarian narrative. It read, in part:

Whereas, ever before in the history of the world has there been a time where men have dared so unblushingly to defy the principles of justice and human reason and seriously attempt to create, protect and support chaos as a social and political institution as have the great and victorious powers and their abominable lackeys – Servia, Roumania, Greece and Bulgaria, in the case of the Balkans since the year 1912; and whereas a careful study of the postwar map of the Balkan peninsula in general, the map of Macedonia in particular, reveals magnificently the skillfully woven web of evil genius, dooming to bondage, privation and servitude millions of human beings, by turning back the hands of the clock of progress and culture, decreeing that in this part of the world, even the most elementary civils rights and liberties, not alone the sacred right of self-determination, shall be denied to the people; and whereas, Macedonia, like Croatia, Ireland, Switzerland, etc., has been for centuries considered, even by its most terrible and ill-tutored rulers, a geographic, economic and historic unit, it has now been divided and dismembered in a most insane manner by allotting to Greece the entire water front along the Aegean.

Now, therefore, be it resolved – That a revision of the treaties of Bucharest, Neuilly and Versailles, dealing with the fate of the Macedonian people and their liberty, happiness and future, be demanded of the powers, signatories of these treaties, so that Macedonia may again belong to its own people, by becoming an autonomous and independent state, if peace in the Balkans is to be attained and the recurrence of further devastory debacles to be avoided.[79]

Aside from the damning accusations against Europe, such as labeling its treatment of Macedonia as a "skillfully woven web of evil genius, dooming to bondage, privation and servitude of millions of human beings," this resolution is notable for three reasons. First, it treats Bulgaria in the same vein as Serbia and Greece. Second, it defines

Macedonia's right to exist (as a separate and independent country) as an economic, geographic and historic right, of which the latter is not much different from the statement by MPO's incorporators who claimed Macedonia's independence was an ancient right. Third, it describes the Macedonian people. While not explicitly saying that the Macedonians comprised their own national, ethnic or racial group, the absence of the term 'Bulgarian' to describe the people is noteworthy, since that would eventually become the norm for the MPO.

This emphasis on Macedonia's unjust division and the plight of the Macedonian people was common in these early years. For example, in April 1928, President Shaneff wrote an editorial for the *Indianapolis Star* regarding the history of Macedonia and its quest for independence. He wrote:

Through such political maneuvers Macedonia was cowardly and maliciously divided among Bulgaria, Greece and Servia after her 'liberation' from Turkey. It is a tradition among the Balkan politicians to plot against each other, and when two or more come to an 'agreement' the third is the poor victim. This tradition was the least profitable for the poor Macedonians, who in their Christian innocence had placed great trust to the promises of their Christian neighbors who pretended 'liberation' but actually planned division of Macedonia. Of such nature are, in our eyes, these agreements made or to be made between Balkan states.

But what is the real cause of the trouble? It is Macedonia, which has been and still is the object of the trouble. Artificial division of Macedonia between Bulgaria, Greece and Servia will not bring friendship among the Balkan states. Nor will it prevent future wars. Indeed, Macedonia is the center of the trouble, which is chiefly based on the enmity, jealousy and the hate of the Balkan states, always ready to make 'agreements' for the division of Macedonia, which for over

thirty years has been fighting for her independence...[C]reation of an autonomous state of Macedonia will put an end to all the controversies, enmities and wars in the turbulent Balkan peninsula. Our organization is working for the same cause.[80]

After Jordan Chkatroff's arrival a few year prior, however, we begin to see the first 'pro-Bulgarian' push, even though it is only used sparingly in these first years. At a June 30, 1925 speech at the Macedono-Bulgarian Orthodox church in Indianapolis, Chkatroff began this normalization of 'Bulgarian' for MPO's agenda:

The situation in Macedonia is characterized by constant anarchy instigated from the highest to the lowest organs of the governing authorities and by a ceaseless tendency to denationalize and uproot the local population which is composed chiefly of Bulgarians, Turks, Roumanians and Albanians. These nationalities are deprived of the most elementary possibilities for cultural developments, because their churches, schools, libraries, editorial offices and others have been closed. And, strange to say, these institutions existed even in the time of the 'unspeakable Turk'.

The Greek government profited off a convention for the exchange of populations, made with the former government of Stambolisky in order to force out Bulgarians from Macedonia. Consequently, they were expelled by the thousands with cruelty in the bitterest cold of winter. At present, these unfortunates are wandering about homeless and naked in the cities of foreign states.[81]

Still, the 'Bulgarian' terminology had not quite rooted itself in MPO's meaning of 'Macedonian' by the time of the 1925 convention, where the primary discussion among the delegates was about how to enlist American assistance in creating a Balkan federation and "obtaining freedom of the

Macedonians." Lazar Kisselincheff stated that the political and academic societies of America were "well aware of the inhuman treatment alleged to have been given the Macedonians and other Balkan peoples," indicating that the Macedonians were one of many types of Balkan peoples. P.D. Zellenlist from Chicago also emphasized the need for a Balkan federation of which Macedonia would be an integral component. He said:

The key to the entire Balkan situation is Macedonia. The sooner the Macedonian question is settled through the creation of an independent republic, the sooner will the hope of the suffering masses in the Balkans be realized. The hope of the Balkans is the creation of a Balkan federation, consisting of all the provinces and states of that section of Europe, creating one great union. For then there will be no bone of contention to disturb the peaceful cultural, social and economic development of the great, neglected and suffering peoples of that part of the world.[82]

Similarly, two months later, Shaneff and Kisselincheff penned an article for the *Indianapolis Star* on behalf of the MPO Central Committee. The term 'Bulgarian' was not mentioned, as we read here:

They parceled our native country into three distinct parts. They destroyed its economic unity and are the cause of the exodus of hundreds of thousands of Macedonia's most brilliant sons. The injustice and violation exercised over the national consciousness of the Macedonian people by being deprived of their most elementary human rights in using their own language, in having their own churches, schools, libraries and cultural institutions, coupled with the tragedy of thousands of Macedonian families dying from cold and hunger across the boundaries in Bulgaria, where they have been forced to seek shelter from Greek and Serbian cruelty and terror, will be almost incredible to those who will write

the story of contemporary history. They will be the blackest pages in the book of civilization in Europe today. ...

At the beginning of a severe winter the Greek artillery and troops have shelled and burned unprotected districts, killed many innocent men, women and children and cause the exodus of an interminable caravan of panic-stricken Macedonian civilians before them. Appealing to its sense of justice the central committee of the Union of the Macedonian Political Organizations of the United States and Canada begs the civilized world to take speedy measures in order to bring to and end this unbearable situation. The Macedonian population should be allowed peacefully to develop and should be guaranteed the application of the clauses for the protection of minorities incorporated in the treaty of Neuilly, which are so cynically overlooked by the present rulers of our divided country.[83]

Some MPO members even referred to their language as Macedonian and not Bulgarian. The MPO branch in Mansfield, 'Ohrid', was led by Mike Christ. In February of 1927, 'Ohrid' presented a play and Christ told the news that "the entire play will be given in the Macedonian language."[84]

Mike Christ, in particular, was an equal opportunist and consistently advocated for the uniqueness of the Macedonians, as evidenced by his historical description of Macedonia to the *News-Journal* in Mansfield:

The Macedonian people were for centuries subjugated under the yoke of Turkish despotism. After the liberalization of the Balkan states – Serbia, Roumania, Greece and Bulgaria, the Macedonians created a strong revolutionary organization known as the Interior Revolutionary Organization, whose motto was, 'Macedonia for Macedonians,' a Monroe doctrine for that overridden country in the South-eastern part of

Europe. This movement swept the country and in 1903 the Ilinden Insurrection broke out and covered the entire Macedonia. It was a struggle for liberty and independence. In the revolution more than 5,000 Macedonians were killed by the Turks and 100,000 refugees fled to the United States, Bulgaria and other Balkan states.

In 1912 the Balkan states formed the well known alliance against Turkey. This alliance resulted in the division of Macedonia and the scattering of Macedonians all over the Balkan Peninsula. By treaty of Bucharest, which followed the second Balkan War in 1913, Macedonia was divided among Serbia, Greece and Bulgaria. This division was confirmed by the treaty of Neuilly in 1919 and now again the Macedonians are without self-government and liberty.[85]

In fact, in these early years, MPO did not hesitate to attack Bulgaria, or differentiate between Bulgarians and Macedonians, particularly when Bulgaria tried to emulate Serbian and Greek tactics in dealing with its Macedonian minority. In May of 1927, MPO's Central Committee protested against Bulgaria's "sale of Macedonian schools, churches and other national possessions to Greece." Shaneff and even Chkatroff signed this protest to Bulgaria on behalf of the MPO, which stated: "Organized Macedonians in America and Canada protest vigorously against the sale of our sacred possessions in Macedonia. We condemn that policy as antinational and anti-Macedonian. The proper owners of these properties are the Macedonian people and no one is authorized to sell them."[86] Clearly, the MPO was more than willing to emphasize the uniqueness of the Macedonian people when the target was Bulgaria. When the MPO attacked Bulgaria, it referred to its schools and people as Macedonians; when the attacks were aimed at Greece or Serbia, however, the term 'Bulgarian' would become more frequent.

For example, in August of 1927, MPO 'Justice', based in Toronto, appealed to the World Federation of Education Associations to "exercise influence" for the solution of the Macedonian Question, and in particular they targeted Greece and Serbia. Their public statement unambiguously referred to the Macedonians as Bulgarians:

Serbia and Greece for their own reasons refuse to apply the treaty stipulations regarding the Bulgarian population in Macedonia and the great powers are silent to the protests of the Macedonians. There will be no true international morality, justice and good-will if the Macedonian question is not solved according to the wish of the Macedonian people, which may be established any time by proper plebiscite under the control of the great powers.[87]

However, in October, when describing the situation in the Balkans for a newspaper, George Popoff of MPO in Dayton, described the language, schools and churches of Macedonians as 'Bulgarian' but the people as Macedonians. This was common for Macedonians before World War II because most Macedonian towns, for reasons dating back to the late Ottoman period, had been under jurisdiction of the Bulgarian Orthodox Church. Unlike MPO in Toronto, however, Popoff did not refer to the population as 'Bulgarian':

The causes for the revolutionary activity are as follows:

1. **The unwillingness of the Serbian government to apply the minority clauses of the Neuilly treaty in Macedonia, where all Bulgarian schools and churches are closed and the use of the Bulgarian language and literature is unreservedly prohibited.**
2. **The unbearable situation in Macedonia, where since May of this year the unprotected population has been**

43

subjected to a terror unknown in the history of Macedonian sufferings, and of the Serbian state up to the present time.

3. The imprisonment of more than 50 Macedonian students at the Universities in Skopje, Zagreb, Lubljana and Belgrade in the filthy, humid underground passages of the Skopje dungeon. The cause of their arrest was that Bulgarian literature was found on them. They are tortured by the severest of inquisition methods, flogging, burning by red-hot iron rods, twisting of the sexual organs, placing of hot boiling eggs under the arms, etc.

The Macedonians, who have repeatedly requested the intervention of the League of Nations for the application of the promised minority rights and which requests were not heeded, either by the League or by Serbia or Greece, have adopted against their will as the only means for the protection of their life, honor and nationality the revolutionary struggle thrust upon them by the Serbian terrorist government.

Popoff further explained that Serbian accusations against Bulgaria for the attacks on the Serbian state were unfounded because it was IMRO and the Macedonians, and not Bulgaria, that were fighting Serbia.[88]

Steelton MPO's branch, 'Prilep', echoed the above sentiments. A.E. Yanchuleff and George Andoff issued a similar statement that referred to literature as Bulgarian but the people as Macedonian:

As a result of these inhumane tortures the students Vangeloff and Hadji Kimoff went insane. Thomas Petroff lies unconscious on his deathbed and Boris Andreeff, having been burned with a red-hot iron on his chest and fingers, was taken out of the city during the night and placed before an open grave with the threat that if he did not disclose the party that spread Bulgarian literature he would be killed. Todor P. Jordanoff, a beneficiary of the Serbian king, aware of the cruel suffering that awaited him in the prison, as soon as he found out that the Serbian police was in his footsteps, threw himself under the wheels of the express train at the station of Zemlin and was killed...The above facts show us once and for all that the Serbian government willingly does not want to listen to the voice of the maltreated Macedonian population.[89]

This critique of the Serbian government quickly caught the attention of Serbian-Americans. A Serbian named Vuckovitch, based in Indianapolis, wrote a scathing attack against the MPO in December of 1927 and questioned the organization's loyalty to the United States. He stated that the MPO was really just an extension of the secretive and terrorist organization known as IMRO. As we know, the IMRO had a large part in helping create the MPO, but the MPO would not be completely under the control of Mihajlov's faction for a few more years. Accordingly, MPO member P.G. Sirmin responded to Vuckovitch's attacks with a vigorously pro-Macedonian perspective:

I am a Macedonian and a member of this Macedonian political organization in Indianapolis, but the organization is not a secret one. Indeed, it is recognized by the government and has a charter for its legal existence. The members are neither communists nor fascists...Because we know how bad are the conditions, we, who were fortunate to get out of Macedonia and to come here, have organized to tell the world about the unbearable conditions under which our unfortunate folks are subjected.

Mr. Vuckovitch, as a Serbian, is trying to defend his country and thus openly becomes a supporter of the Serbian King and his government. Macedonians in this country do not like the Serbian King. We like this republic and declare our loyalty

unreserved...There is no crime to organize in order to expose the inhuman tortures which the Macedonians suffer. In Serbia this crime is perhaps punishable with death, but, thank God, we are not living in Serbia.[90]

The MPO assault on the Serbian state, and the confrontations between Macedonians and Serbs, only increased. At the 1928 MPO convention in Detroit, Kisselincheff repeated the "demand that the Balkans be formed into a federation of states after the manner of the United States, with Macedonia as a sovereign unit." If that failed, he warned: "So long as Macedonia is not free and independent, Macedonian nationalities will continue their struggle to liberate their fatherland." That same day, however, there was a Serbian rally a few miles away at the Serbian Orthodox Church. Drake Alles Manduschich blasted MPO and some of their statements suggesting Macedonians were a separate people: "To lie, bluff and parade in the United States about an independent Macedonia is absurd...This revolutionary gang abuses the hospitality of America and is creating disturbances, murders and robberies in southern Serbia." He continued: "There is no such thing as a Macedonian race. There is no such country as Macedonia. They are Serbs in Macedonia. Macedonia is not an administrative unit that ever had a political or social order."[91]

Still, that did not rattle the MPO leaders. At the convention, Christ Anastasoff, who would go on to be a prolific author and MPO advocate, made a speech to the large crowd.

Macedonia, the land of our birth, is now divided among Bulgaria, Servia and Greece without the consent of the people. In Macedonia under Servia and Greece the governments and their agents are able to rule only by force and despotism which seek to destroy the rights of the

Macedonians to choose their government. Even under the bloodiest of the Turkish rulers, 'Red' Sultan Hamid, the Macedonians had some rights. Under Servia and Greece they have none...All the suppressing measures used by Servia and Greece aim at but one thing: to force Macedonia to undeserved submission and capitulation.

What is the result? The country is an open revolution the people is fighting to remove from its throat the criminal grip that chokes the defenseless and misfortunate folks. In this fight the people are right...If we are to gain freedom for Macedonia on false pretenses we prefer to tell the truth. Macedonia will be free and happy when the truth is known. In the struggle for independence, the Macedonian people have only one trusted and dependable weapon – the truth and with that they expect to win.[92]

Even as late as 1929, the abundantly pro-Macedonian stance and absence of pro-Bulgarian sentiment was clear. MPO 'Prilep' in Steelton issued their own statement lambasting Serbian rule in March, and it highlighted the Macedonians as a nation and a people. The appeal stated:

The Macedonians residing in the United States and Canada have carried a legal struggle under the banner of their union of Macedonian Political Organizations of United States and Canada for years and now the Croatians of America put the foundations of their own union for a definite and systematic national struggle for liberty and independence of their Fatherland-Croatia. The Macedonian and Croatian unions therefore find at this point the identity of their aspirations and by this common appeal to all country-loving Croatians and Macedonians in America they establish the firm cooperation against the common foe...The Macedonians have carried on this struggle for a long time – and now the Croatians have joined. This is the struggle for the salvation, liberty and happy future of our brotherly relations. Let us thicken our ranks wherever we are...Our struggle is not for

47

authority but it is the struggle for the most elementary human rights and for the invincible truth. The liberty-loving and justice-loving world is with us.[93]

Around this same time, however, we begin to see an open shift to Mihajlov and his brand of Macedonian identity. Chkatroff, in a speech, made a subtle but significant show of support for Mihajlov by labeling him as the leader of the "true" revolutionary force in Macedonia. Chkatroff made this statement after highlighting Serbia and Greece's oppressive regimes:

I must, with regret, say that a part of the public in western Europe and the United States, on account of lack of information on the actual conditions in Macedonia and the cruelty of the Serbian and Greek regimes, has taken a negative attitude toward the revolutionary struggle of the Macedonians considering the latter as the troublemakers and advising them to take resort to legal methods for attainment of their goal...Our tragedy, however, is found in the injustice of international treaties which determine the fate of Macedonia. This is the source of all sufferings for the Balkan populations and the cause for all the troubles in southeastern Europe...In Macedonia we have not the right to speak our mother tongue; to pray to our God in our mother tongue and to school ourselves in it. Our churches, schools and libraries have been closed. Part of the intellectuals have been slaughtered, another part is dying away in dungeons and under cruel torture, and still another is in exile...

No one can demand from the Macedonians their self-annihilation or an unresisting acceptance of injustice and tyranny. The final aim of the struggle is to win complete political independence for Macedonia within its geographic and economic borders. This is the safest guarantee for Balkan peace and this is the first requirement for a bigger state integrity in the Balkan peninsula, as will be expressed in a federation of Balkan states and will work for the speedy and final liquidation of the old animosities, revolutions and bloodshed among the Balkan people. The interior Macedonian revolutionary organizations today is more powerful, more lively and more active than at any time in the past. The new central committee, consisting of Ivan Michailoff, Ivan Karadjioff, and Strahil Razvigoroff, elected unanimously at the seventh regular congress of the organization, enjoys the complete confidence of the true Macedonian revolutionary forces and directs the liberation causes of oppressed Macedonians safely.[94]

This, unfortunately, was the beginning of MPO's shift to Mihajlov's faction, and it signals the start of a more forceful and open 'Bulgarian' description of the Macedonians. For example, in April of 1930, Naum Bitsoff, secretary of the Cincinnati MPO branch, wrote an editorial on the situation in Macedonia and Balkans. He wastes no time in calling the Macedonians 'Bulgarian':

The Macedonians, which in their majority are of Bulgarian origin, were deprived of all their national rights and liberation by the Governments of Belgrade and Athens. Serbia and Greece certainly knew that the Macedonians, chiefly the Bulgarians of Macedonia, who carried on, many decades before the World War, a strong fight for gaining of their national liberty, would not accept the new yoke, determined for them by the victorious Powers in Paris. They knew that the Macedonians will raise up a protest and will fight again, if it were necessary, to obtain freedom. ...

They decided not to accord any of the minority rights to the Bulgarians in the respective parts of Macedonia, as it is provided in the minority clauses of the treaties of peace. They expected thus to cut short with the question of the national cultural rights of the Bulgarian minorities in Macedonia. Indeed, they refused to recognize the existence of Bulgarian population in their states, despite the fact that in their two parts of Macedonia live about 1,500,000 Bulgarians. In one

49

word, Serbia and Greece proceeded to a total extermination of the Bulgarians in Macedonia under their domination...We, the Macedonians, are from inside the country. We have our relatives there and are in close connection with everything that happens in Macedonia. We can, therefore, tell something more and really true about the Serbian rule in Macedonia...In Macedonia the forced Serbianization is carried out by most inhuman means. The Belgrade Government closed there all Bulgarian schools, churches, libraries and other Bulgarian cultural institutions; banished the Bulgarian teachers, bishops, priests and other intellectual workers; many of them were arrested and killed by the agents of the authorities.

The Macedonian Bulgarians are forbidden in their own country to speak and read Bulgarian books and newspapers. Even the Holy Bible they cannot read in their mother tongue. Belgrade put in execution most drastic measures in order to exterminate the Bulgarian people in Jugoslavian part of Macedonia. Naturally the Macedonians answered with a double resistance. Thus initiated bitter struggle between the new rulers of that country and the conquered population. A struggle for life or death – on the part of the Macedonians. Having been deprived of all means for a legal struggle, the Macedonians in Macedonia had to resort to force of arms in order to gain their rights: -- peace and liberty at home. In the name of the same aim the Macedonians abroad organized a struggle by legal means...It is not true at all, that the aim of the IMRO is to bring about a war between Bulgaria and Jugoslavia. The aim of the IMRO is to liberate Macedonia, dragging down the tyranny of the Serbian and Greek Governments.[95]

That year, the MPO convention was held in Youngstown, Ohio. Here, they presented the League of Nations with two political resolutions that criticized the Greek and Yugoslavian governments for their heavy-handed rule in their respective parts of Macedonia. In accordance with the new 'pro-Bulgarian' attitude of the MPO, the MPO Central Committee stated they were submitting these resolutions "on behalf of the Bulgarians in Macedonia."[96]

Similarly, in 1930, Shaneff took a more pro-Bulgarian stance. Before the MPO internal strife, Shaneff had been more closely aligned with Zografoff and other left-leaning Macedonians. Shaneff had generally shied away from calling the Macedonian people 'Bulgarians.' But now he increasingly attached the Bulgarian label to the Macedonian people, as shown in this article he wrote for *Indianapolis Star* that focused on problems in Greece:

Greece of today does not respect the liberty of national conscience for any of the other nationalities but the Greeks in Macedonia. By drawing attention to this fact, we, the Macedonians of the United States and Canada, numbering over forty-five thousand, are fulfilling our duty towards truth and humanity. Our country has been divided among Greece, Serbia (so-called Jugoslavia) and Bulgaria...We are very well acquainted with life in contemporary Greece. We have experienced the tyranny and the cruelty of its rule. We are conscious of our origin as Bulgarians, Aroumanians (Kutso-Vlachs) and Turks, and we cannot help but suffer with the ones that have been left behind. Greece is trying to assimilate us. ...

Under this unbearable tyranny, which is even worse than the Turkish was, the Macedonian population has no legal means of securing its rights and so it is forced through revolutionary methods to adopt a system of bombing affairs and political assassinations....The ideal of Macedonia is to make out of her three parts one autonomous state in which different nationalities can live brotherly and freely...To prove what we have stated above, we are prepared to accept an investigation by representatives of the League of Nations or other international institutions.[97]

51

The Greeks in Indianapolis reacted to Shaneff's statement by calling it "untruthful, insincere and false." Shaneff then responded in another editorial, reinforcing that by 'Macedonian' the MPO really meant 'Bulgarian'.

Another point is the question concerning the Bulgarian schools and churches, closed by the Greek authorities in Macedonia. The three Greeks say that the Bulgarian church is orthodox, the same as the Greek church. That is true, too. But – here must be put another "but" – the Macedonian Bulgarians want the language of their church to be Bulgarian, not Greek, as the case was under the Turkish rule in Macedonia twenty years ago. Because they do not know the Greek language. The same is the case with the Bulgarian schools in Macedonia. ...

The central committee of the Macedonian political organization in this country and Canada, the main purpose of which is to call the public attention to the thorny and troublesome Macedonian question and thus contribute to the betterment of the conditions in the Balkans, considers its duty to be to emphasize that Greece is proceeding to apply inhuman, barbarous means in order to annihilate or expatriate the Bulgarians from Greece.[98]

Still, some MPO members remained fairly consistent in their insistence that Macedonians were their own people. Paul G. Sirmin, who had written an enthusiastically pro-Macedonian article in 1927, wrote another article in August of 1932 in response to an editorial in the *Indianapolis Star* that stated Macedonians were Serbs. Sirmin insisted that Macedonians are not Serbs and constitute their own people:

The Macedonians have nothing in common with the Serbians. They were never Serbians, are not now and never will be. If anybody knows or ought to know about the Macedonians and their nationalities and their consciousness, the most proper ones to know would be the Macedonians themselves. Furthermore, Macedonia, in proportion to her population, produces more professors, scholars, diplomats, lawyers, doctors, writers, artists, technicians, teachers and journalists than any other Balkan nation, and in spite of intolerable political conditions.

The Serbians seem to think they will make 'old Serbians' out of the Macedonians by torture and death. If the Macedonians are the old-pure-straight-Serbians, as Mr. Nikolin would have you believe, why did the Serbs terrorize the Macedonians with the so-called 'black hand' immediately after they invaded Macedonia? ...

The Macedonians are organized everywhere and are ready and willing to give any and all information relative to the history of the Macedonian people. We are fighting for liberty and righteousness. The Macedonian demand natural and God-given rights for themselves and all other nations. They ask for nothing that does not belong to them.[99]

However, Sirmin seems to have been a minority voice amongst MPO's leaders during this shift to Mihajlovism. For example, in April of 1933, the MPO Central Committee issued a statement accusing Serbia of suppressing "all Bulgarian cultural institutions" and of having "now set about exterminating the Bulgars who remained in [Macedonia] and eradicating prominent Bulgarian families who had taken part in the struggle for political and economic liberty."[100] The MPO official stance was becoming increasingly adamant that Macedonians were indeed Bulgarians.

Even when the MPO attacked the Bulgarian government in July of 1934, the MPO referred to the Macedonians as

Bulgarians and compatriots to Bulgaria's Bulgarians. The distinction between Macedonians and Bulgarians was not highlighted as it had been in the 1920s. One MPO statement on the issue read:

The central committee of the Macedonian Political Organization of the United States and Canada, in the name of tens of thousands of Bulgarians from Macedonia, expresses its deep affliction of the way your government treats our compatriots there. We demand your intervention and for the release of all arrested and interned Macedonians and the punishment of all responsible organs of your government for the assaults and arbitrariness of the people in the Petrichko and Kustendilsko provinces. The state of siege in these provinces is a black spot in the government of your prime minister, and the enlightened world energetically opposes such ways of terror.[101]

Later that year, a declaration from MPO's convention was submitted to the *Detroit Free Press* by Christ Anastasoff, who was now president of MPO 'Fatherland' in Detroit. The resolution continued to use the terms 'Bulgars', 'Bulgarians' and 'Macedonians' interchangeably. In part, the declaration stated:

Through a brutal regime the Governments of Belgrade and Athens purport to destroy the wakeful consciousness of the Macedonian Bulgars. The methods applied in this connection can be described only as barbaric. Since 1918, the Macedonian people, especially those of Bulgarian origin, which comprise the bulk of the population, continue to live under an indescribably martyrdom.[102]

At the same time, however, the declaration managed to attack Bulgaria (in addition to Serbia and Greece) for impeding the Macedonian Cause. Interestingly, this coincides with Bulgaria's change in power and pursuit of eradicating Bulgaria (and particular Pirin Macedonia) of Mihajlov's IMRO faction. The declaration continued:

Pointing out the ruthless regimes existing in those parts of Macedonia under Serb and Greek domination, we cannot but call the attention also of all enlightened people, to the grave conditions prevailing since May 19 this year in that part of Macedonia under Bulgarian jurisdiction, which is inhabited by some 200,00 Macedonians. The present dictatorship government in Bulgaria in its desire to suppress the Macedonian cause has undertaken without any legal basis whatsoever, a fierce and unjustifiable persecution of our brothers and sisters in the section of our Fatherland as well as of the half a million Macedonian immigrants in Bulgaria itself.

Hundreds of Macedonians have been arrested, many have been interned, and the Macedonian press, such of it as exists, is subjected to a strict and unlawful censorships...Understanding and rapprochement among the Balkan nations can be possible only through a just gratification of the lawful Macedonian demands – that is, the union of the three severed parts of our Fatherland into a free and independent state.[103]

Moreover, when the notorious IMRO assassin Vlad Chernozemsky assassinated the Serbian king in France, the MPO enthusiastically embraced the news. At a 1936 MPO event in Windsor, Canada honoring the anniversary of the assassination, Chernozemsky was called "the greatest Macedonian of them all" by George Nicoloff, who was reverend at the Macedonian-Bulgarian Orthodox Church 'St. Clement Ohridski' in metro-Detroit. The Windsor branch even decided to name itself after Chernozemsky in the assassin's honor. I.K. Bezoff, official of the Windsor group, stated: "It is not that we love bloodshed, but if bloodshed is necessary to freedom, it is. Many people do not understand our making a hero of an assassin, but to us Alexander was a tyrant...We can give only our moral support, from this distance, but Macedonians never will give up until Macedonia for her own people becomes a reality.[104] While this does not highlight a necessarily pro-Bulgarian view of the Macedonians, it demonstrates how attached the MPO was to Mihajlov's IMRO, even after it was disbanded and exiled from all Balkan countries in the late 1930s.

Bezoff actually never outright called the Macedonians 'Bulgarians'. He labeled the Macedonian tongue as 'Bulgarian', for reasons already explained; but to him, the Macedonians were just Macedonians, as evidenced in his description of the conditions of Macedonia after he returned from a Balkan trip. His praise from IMRO, however, is not masked:

From the time John Metaxas took over the governing power in Greece some 14 months ago, he has subjected Macedonians speaking the Bulgarian tongue to a terror not remembered even under the Turkish yoke. Even the unjust Neuilly Treaty of 1919 guaranteed the right to Macedonians to continue to use their own language. Yet, in my recent visit to that part of Macedonia under Greece I have seen with my own eyes persons 60 years of age and over fined and imprisoned because they dared to speak their mother tongue – the only tongue they could converse in. ...

I am not a member of the Macedonian revolutionary organization known as IMRO, which was founded in 1893. This organization fights within Macedonia against Macedonian oppressors and is responsible for uprisings against them. On the other hand, there is a different type of movement, namely, Macedonian Political organization...which was founded some 16 years ago. ...

Our movement, the MPO, is carrying on in full harmony with the existing laws within the respective countries where it is established, and the activities of the MPO are not revolutionary, but only by way of pen and speech to bring to the attention of the world the oppression in the country of our birth.[105]

Over the next couple of years, we see a slight shift away from the pro-Bulgarian attitude. At the 1937 MPO convention, Toronto's chapter 'Justice' delivered a message to the Central Committee: "Macedonians! We, your countrymen in Toronto, organized into the powerful MPO [local] 'Justice' send you our greetings and salutations. Let us work in unison for the attainment of a free and independent Macedonia which has been the goal of our fathers and benefactors. We wish you all a successful convention. Let us hope that the next one is held in the capital of our country – Salonica – on the Aegean Sea. Long Live Macedonia!"[106]

Then, in May of 1938, the MPO sent a note of protest to Bulgaria's Prime Minister, George Kioseivanov. It demanded "the release of Macedonian political prisoners in Bulgaria and freedom for the suppressed Macedonian press in that country."[107] After the MPO convention in Buffalo that year, a resolution was issued that stated: "In the name of justice and truth, support our just demand for the execution of an impartial international investigation in the three sections of our disjoined and enslaved Motherland...the unspeakable and atrocious cruelty to which the peace-loving Macedonian people are subjected by the governments of Greece and Jugoslavia constitute a serious threat to the peace of the Balkans."[108] Without a base of operations for IMRO, it seemed as if the MPO was beginning to lose faith in the Bulgarian conscience.

57

World War II soon started and the MPO became relatively quiet. Bulgaria allied with the Nazis, which made it difficult for MPO in the United States, who was fighting against the Nazis, to take a pro-Bulgarian approach, even when it was rumored and acknowledged that Mihajlov had made deals with the Nazis. When asked why Mihajlov sided with Hitler and the Nazis, Mihajlov's wife, Menka, spoke frankly about IMRO's opportunism:

We have learned at last not to see around the corner of the future. Today we deal with today's enemies in Macedonia, without a thought of tomorrow. And tomorrow we will take a fresh start and deal with the enemies of tomorrow. Right now the devil himself would be a welcome ally in Macedonia's war of liberation.[109]

It would have been hard for many Macedonians – whether in MPO or not – to publicly support joining with Hitler and the Nazis in order to achieve an independent Macedonia. Many MPO members were also proud Americans; an MPO officially promoting such line of reasoning could have occasioned its demise. Thus, MPO was careful to relax its rhetoric during the war years.

Other Macedonians distanced themselves from the MPO during this time; or if they remained within the MPO, they towed a very pro-Macedonian line so not to appear pro-Hitler, who was aligned with Bulgaria's fascists. For example, during Ilinden celebrations in Akron in 1941, Nick Dosheff (who was vice-president of the Akron MPO chapter in the mid-1920s)[110] stated: "We Macedonian-Americans strongly condemn the Nazi regime and Nazi domination of Balkans as true Americans pledge our support to our government and its foreign policy in trying to stop the spread of what is perhaps the worst plague in the world today."[111] Four years earlier, however, Dosheff was only eager to express the Bulgarian character of the Macedonians, saying that there was "no Macedonian language" and that "we are a Slav race by right, but Bulgarian by nationality."[112]

After the war ended, the MPO saw an opportunity to create an independent Macedonia that could potentially be under the protection of the United States and other Western powers. In April of 1944, Macedonians in Akron met to "draw up a plea to President Roosevelt for the liberation of [Macedonia]." "We are looking forward with great enthusiasm and hope for the application of the principles of the Atlantic charter for the benefit of oppressed nations such as Macedonia," said John Mitseff. "Centuries of oppression haven't been able to stamp out Macedonian culture, customs and speech. It shall never be stamped out, and such a determined fight for what is rightfully theirs can only end in victory."[113] The resolution to Roosevelt was 16 pages and stated that Macedonia was "divided and subjugated by the regimes of three neighboring countries – Yugoslavia, Bulgaria and Greece – and its people now live under Hitler's Nazi rule."[114] The MPO made sure they appeared as pro-American as possible in their attempts to advocate for a free and independent Macedonia.

Of course, however, this shift was not permanent. MPO would continue advocating for a 'Macedonia for the Macedonians' and would continue being patriotic Americans. But they soon began assuming a staunchly anti-Yugoslavian and pro-Bulgarian agenda. This would have severe consequences not only for the MPO as an organization, but also for the general Macedonian Cause.

Part II: The True Face

THREE
Anti-Communism and Pro-Bulgarianism

Upon the completion of World War II, Vardar Macedonia became incorporated in Tito's Yugoslavia as a constituent republic, along with Slovenia, Croatia, Bosnia & Hercegovina, Serbia, and Montenegro. Although not independent or united, Macedonia was finally recognized as an equal to its fellow Balkan neighbors. Bulgaria's new regime was even in discussions with Yugoslavia to add its part of Macedonia, Pirin Macedonia, to the republic of Macedonia in Yugoslavia upon the creation of a Balkan confederation. Macedonians in Greece, meanwhile, were agitating for independence (and likely would have won it had it not been for British and American intervention and support for Greece's kingdom) in anticipation of uniting all of Macedonia.

Irrespective of Macedonians' aspirations, the reality was that they had their own republic and were recognized as a nation and ethnic group. Moreover, the Macedonian language was soon codified and in a couple of decades the Macedonian Orthodox Church would declare its independence from the Serbian Orthodox Church. Most Macedonians were euphoric: their dreams were partly realized and their struggles were not wasted. There was a lot of work to do, but the world was finally embracing the Macedonian nation as reality.

It is telling, then, that the MPO was adamantly opposed to this new reality for the Macedonians. MPO had been aligned with the right-wing IMRO through the 1930s and

1940s, and most of its leaders were rooting for Mihajlov and right-wing Macedonians in defeating the Macedonian Partisans, who were staving off Bulgarian, German, Italian and Albanian occupiers. Many of these pro-Bulgarian Macedonians were chased out of Macedonia or had fled because Tito's Yugoslavia pursued a campaign to punish traitors who had aligned with the fascist Bulgarian army and Mihajlov's IMRO. For example, Cyril Johns (Kyril Evanoff), the father of future MPO president Chris Evanoff, fled Macedonia in 1944 because he knew "he would be in trouble for his outspoken views." He left three days before Macedonian Communists came to his house and allegedly killed his father.[115]

The Macedonians had a Macedonian language, a nation, a church, and recognition as a separate people, and the MPO opposed all of it. They insisted that they spoke Bulgarian and were ethnic Bulgarians, and they remained adherents of the Bulgarian Orthodox Church. They still advocated for a united Macedonia, but the concept of a Balkan Federation was no longer as desirable to them (even though it was ironic, as Yugoslavia was a type of Balkan federation), and the MPO now insisted only independence for Macedonia.

Luben Dimitroff, the editor of the *Macedonian Tribune* and the man who the CIA believed served as the direct link between Ivan Mihajlov and the MPO, began turning the *Tribune* into an anti-communism vehicle, specifically an anti-Yugoslavian mouthpiece. In September of 1945, he wrote an editorial for the *Indianapolis News*, where he rejected Yugoslavia as Macedonia's hope and suggested Macedonia should be separated from Yugoslavia and given independence. He further said that "during the last three decades, four wars occurred in the Balkans, all of them inspired by aspirations for Macedonian territory. ... I suggest that the best solution of the knotty Macedonian problem may be achieved by adopting and applying the popular motto of the Macedonian people: Macedonia for the Macedonians."[116] MPO's leaders were quickly distancing themselves from Yugoslavia and the Macedonian nation recognized under this restructured country.

Thus, at the 1947 convention in Indianapolis, the MPO drafter a letter to the United Nations asking it to create and protect an independent and united Macedonia. This letter detailed how that could happen:

1. Best method of removing hate among Yugoslavia, Bulgaria and Greece over Macedonia is to take the question out of their hands.

2. To accomplish the first aim, it is necessary to create an independent democratic political unit within Macedonia.

3. Capital of the Macedonian state should be Salonica, and all Balkan states should be given rights there for export and import trade.

4. The new state should be placed under protection of the UN Security Council.

5. An internationally protected plebiscite should be held.[117]

This appeal was not seriously considered by the world powers. Still, the MPO persisted with this stance. Christ Anastasoff iterated the need for an independent Macedonia under international supervision at the 1949 MPO convention in Fort Wayne:

With an independent state of Macedonia, an end will be put to the century-old Balkan antagonism and wars, primarily struggles of the domination of Macedonia. ... If, for one

reason or another, it will be impossible to take immediate steps toward the formation by which, of course, all democratic rights and liberties would be granted to the citizens of the constituent nationalities. Later on, under the supervision of United Nations organs and an absolute guarantee of impartiality, a national plebiscite could determine the future organization of independent Macedonia. Only those who fear the truth, hate freedom and entertain intentions of conquest would be opposed to our modest suggestions.[118]

Soon, the MPO and *Macedonian Tribune* shouldered an aggressive offensive against Yugoslavia. In 1952, the MPO passed a resolution opposing "all forms of Communism, including those under Tito in Yugoslavia and Chervenkov in Bulgaria."[119] Although Bulgaria's communists were criticized, the MPO rarely challenged the Bulgarian regime in the same way it targeted Yugoslavia. For example, in October of 1956, the MPO released a detailed and scathing attack against Yugoslavia:

1. The present regime in Yugoslavia is communistic. For the last 12 years it has deprived the various people in the country of all their human rights. In Yugoslavia Macedonia things have gone from bad to worse by forcing fatal communistic experiments in a poverty-stricken region.

2. While Moscow is giving outward signs of denouncing the so-called 'personality cult', Belgrade still stands on the old Cominform position; now, more than ever, the cult toward Tito is being cultivated. Tito is the law. When high ranking Communists as Djilas and Dedier find themselves ostracized because of their mild criticism against the regime, one can imagine what the fate of the common man would be, if one dares to declare himself against Tito.

3. There has never been a real and permanent relaxation of Tito's regime toward the people. The fact that Tito has given permission to a few foreign correspondents to visit the country does not mean that democracy is gaining ground in Yugoslavia. The ever-hated UDBA (secret police) is still dreaded everywhere in Yugoslavia.

4. The Free World is aghast at the rate of which people, week after week, are fleeing the one-man regime in Communist Yugoslavia...

5...Tito's representatives have been heavily leaning on the side of Soviet Russia and her satellites.

6. Finally, Tito himself on many occasions has declared that he is a Communist and that he does not intend to change his political Marx-Leninist doctrine.

The resolution then further declared:

1. Any help...given to Tito by the United States should be stopped. We most sincerely congratulate all members of Congress in Washington who have had the courage of taking a strong stand against Tito and his regime...

2. Naïve illusion is to expect Tito to dent the Communist Front. That will never happen.

3. We should always remember that Communists respect power. Tito is no exception. The stronger America is, the more she will be respected and the more the changes for war will be on the diminishing side...

4. Economic aid, however, to the various peoples in Yugoslavia is not only recommended, but it would be a wise step in a right direction, provided this help is distributed by American representatives on the spot where needed...[120]

Further, the Bulgarian character of the MPO and the *Macedonian Tribune* was detailed in a 1956 interview of Luben Dimitroff and Christo Nizamoff (*Tribune* editors) for the *Indianapolis Star*. The *Tribune* was classified as a newspaper "printed in the centuries-old Bulgarian language." "Our system is very simple," said Nizamoff. "We cannot divulge the means, of course – its simplicity has made it so successful that we cannot endanger it." Luben Dimitroff explained: "We are the focal point of these people. Letters come to us daily from all over the free world from people whose ties with the homeland now are broken...We publish many books in both English and Bulgarian. ...If we can reunite our country, it will no longer be a bone of contention for its neighbors. ...We stand on the principle that every country in the Balkans must be free to express itself in a free way as we do here in the United States."[121]

Moreover, in 1958, the MPO adopted a resolution designating October 11 as a "Day of Mourning". This was the first of many resolutions and observances of October 11 as a day for mourning during the following decades. According to Nizamoff, this was a form of protest against the "tyranny in Yugoslavia." In Yugoslavia, the people recognized October 11 as the day that Macedonians began their symbolic struggle against Bulgarian and Nazi fascist occupation.[122] However, for the MPO, this day marked the beginning of the loss of Bulgarian rule in Macedonia and the beginning of the end for Bulgarian propaganda in Macedonia.

It was not just MPO's Central Committee and *Tribune* editors who observed this 'Day of Mourning'. The Alton (Illinois) MPO branch did so as well. Theodore Tchoukaleff described the unverifiable MPO stance that Macedonians were being forced to celebrate their liberation. He said:

Peasants and city folks will be forced to attend the gatherings to listen to endless and monotonous speeches, eulogizing Marx-Leninism and, of course, dictator Tito. Among other things, these meetings will serve the purpose also of impressing foreign observers and visitors, who may happen to be there at the moment, that the Macedonian people are enthusiastically endorsing the Communist way of life. There would be nothing more misleading than such as assumption. Communism has never had any roots in Yugoslav Macedonia. In a country rich with religious and cultural traditions, only brutal force can keep the Communist regime still functioning.[123]

The MPO had clearly established links with Indiana's newspapers and managed to thus get the *Indianapolis News* to pen an editorial in October of 1962 joining the MPO in observing this day of mourning. The editorial board wrote:

Eighteen years ago yesterday the Macedonians inside Yugoslavia became a part of Tito's Red abattoir. Because they are a spirited, liberty-loving people who still view themselves as part of a separate nation, they have suffered more than other Yugoslav nationals at Tito's hands...We who know and respect the Macedonians in Indianapolis are of a more informed opinion. Their protests and their constant underground warfare against Yugoslavia's Red regime are a real and present threat to Tito and his gang...They are brave, unrelenting actionists inside and outside Yugoslavia...The News joins the Macedonian Patriotic Organization of Indianapolis in observing, not only a particular day in October, but all days, as a time of mourning for enslaved freedom fighters.[124]

When Yugoslavia's leader Tito visited the U.S. for the first time in October of 1963, the MPO officially protested this visit. An MPO resolution stated that U.S. aid and recognition of Tito would damage the prestige of the United States. A Macedonian from Pittsburgh by the name of George Dalson led the protest. He said that Tito was using U.S. money to "undermine the position of the Free World in favor of international communism."[125]

Again in 1964 the MPO issued a statement about October 11, as this seemed to be the only political coverage that U.S. media would give the MPO. The statement said that October 11 "is the day the Tito Communist regime liberated the people of most of their human rights, their personal security, their privileges and of all justice." In Ohio, MPO members held a protest meeting in Cincinnati at the home of Anton and James Popov. Anton stated: "We know that someday Tito will fight us with the money we are giving him." He explained that the current purpose of MPO was to see an end to U.S. aid to Tito. "The free world must cut all aid and support of the Communist regimes which came to power mainly through foreign help. Instead of helping the Communists, let the free world extend a helping hand to the oppressed people in Europe."[126]

The free world, however, was generally not in sync with the MPO. In addition to the CIA's recognition of MPO's connection to Mihajlov and his fascist agenda, the Canadian Government became suspicious of the MPO in the 1950s "because of its pro-Bulgarian orientation and its hostility to Greece and Yugoslavia which were Canadian allies in the fight against Communism." On April 9, 1953, Canadian Secretary of State for External Affairs, L.B. Pearson, wrote Charles Henry, a MP for Toronto-Rosedale, regarding his closeness with Reverend Vasil Mihailov, a Macedono-

Bulgarian priest and MPO member, as well as a Bulgarian nationalist. Pearson wrote:

It is naturally not for us at this time to take sides on the complex issues dividing the various Macedonian groups. In particular, we would not wish to appear to show friendliness towards a group which, though apparently anti-Communist, is pro-Bulgarian and hostile to Greece, a country with which we maintain the friendliest relations and with which we are allied in NATO, and Yugoslavia, a country whose continual survival against Soviet pressure is in the general interests of peace and security. I am sure you will appreciate my desire not to extend too friendly a hand to an organization wishing to bring charges - perhaps unfounded and certainly hostile - against our ally Greece.[127]

The MPO began losing significant momentum in the 1950s and 1960s. Their stances found them out of touch with both the American public and the Macedonian people. This 'pro-Macedonia' and 'pro-Bulgarian' stance placed the MPO in direct opposition to the majority of the Macedonians, causing the organization many problems through the next several decades.

FOUR
MPO's Decline

In early April of 1948, a riot broke out at Steelton's Annunciation Macedono-Bulgarian Orthodox Church. George Patoff, who had been chair of a special meeting, "was attempting to read a letter received from a priest in Bulgaria who had been invited to the pastorate of the local church." The letter revealed that the priest, Christo Mitzeff, was an IMRO and MPO supporter. IMRO and MPO were "blamed in some circles for having helped pave the way for Bulgaria's joining with Hitler in World War II." Mitzeff's letter further exposed that some members of the Annunciation congregation had been well informed on the Bulgarian priest's political views and "had worked actively to bring about the bid to Mitzeff without sharing this knowledge with the rest of the congregation." This revelation induced a brawl and over 50 individuals were soon rumbling in the church pews.[128] George Minoff, 51 years old and the former president of the Steelton MPO branch,[129] had shot and killed Koche Atzeff, 24, and Boris Miaff, 30.[130]

For nearly two decades, Steelton's Macedonian community had been divided between those who were in MPO and those were anti-MPO. This division resulted in the majority of the non-MPO members splintering from the Annunciation Church and forming the first Macedonian-American Orthodox Church in the country. However, when the reverend of that church, David Nakoff, died, the non-MPO Macedonians returned to Annunciation. However, the MPO faction was staunchly pro-Bulgarian while the non-

MPO members were trying to disassociate themselves from Bulgarian politics. This splintering led to the fatal shooting of the two Macedonians in the church by MPO loyalist George Minoff.[131]

Fights, stabbings and riots between MPO members and ethnic Macedonians were common throughout MPO's entire existence, both before and after this tragic day. However, this event dealt MPO's image a severe blow in the Macedonian-American community and was one of many reasons the MPO soon found itself in decline. The Pennsylvania courts found Minoff guilty of murder,[132] and the Macedonian masses began realizing that the MPO was guilty of being anti-Macedonian.

MPO's official membership peaked in the mid-1930s at just under 2,000 members.[133] Through the mid-1950s, that number would stay relatively steady. By the end of 1950 there were 1,922 members;[134] in 1951 there were 1,980 members;[135] in 1952 there were 1,986 members;[136] and in 1953 there were 1,980 members.[137] Starting in 1954, the steady decline became noticeable: 1,962 members in 1954;[138] 1,943 members in 1956;[139] and 1,894 members in 1959.[140]

For the first time in nearly 30 years MPO's membership had fallen below 1,900. It would only get worse, however. At the end of 1967, the same year the Macedonian Orthodox Church declared independence, MPO's membership dipped below 1,500.[141] Moreover, starting in the 1970s and through the 1980s, until non-profit organizations in Indiana were no longer required to list their total membership, the MPO would continuously list its membership as exactly 1,500.

The reasons for this decline are many and varied, but essentially revolve around MPO's refusal to orient itself as an ethnic Macedonian organization and instead insistence that it was a Bulgarian organization that supported an independent Macedonia. For example, at the 1956 convention, the bylaws of the MPO was changed to indicate the following: "The terms 'Macedonians' and 'Macedonian immigrants' used in this by-laws pertain equally to all nationality groups in Macedonia – Bulgarians, Arumanians, Turks, Albanians and others." This edit came as a reaction to the increasing number of Macedonians identifying as ethnic Macedonian.[142] The bylaws purposely left out ethnic Macedonians as a group of people in Macedonia – to the MPO, ethnic Macedonians could not possibly exist. This essentially ruined the MPO's credibility.

Of course, other anti-Macedonian statements and acts aroused suspicions and turned people away. In a booklet called *A Visit to Yugoslav Macedonia*, Christ Anastasoff proclaimed that "until 1944 no one has ever heard of such nonsense as a 'Macedonian language' or a 'Macedonian nation.'"[143] For the Macedonians in MPO who considered themselves part of the Macedonian nation who spoke the Macedonian language, this was repulsive. For those newcomers to North America, there was no sense in joining a Bulgarian organization.

Further, at 38th MPO convention in Chicago in 1959, the MPO issued a declaration called 'In Defense of the Bulgarian Orthodox Church in Macedonia'. The MPO renounced Yugoslavia's attempts to create a "Macedonian Orthodox Church in the Old Bulgarian capital city of Ohrid, the Bulgarian Jerusalem."[144] In 1966, the MPO's annual Indiana State filings, for the first time, declared that the purpose of the MPO was to "work for the religious and cultural development of the Americans of Macedonian-Bulgarian descent."[145] Prior to this, the state filings generally talked about Americans of Macedonian descent and 'Bulgarian' was never mentioned.

When, in the 1960s, the Bulgarian government changed its official views regarding Macedonians and stopped acknowledging that a Macedonian ethnicity and language existed, the MPO eagerly welcomed this move. The MPO Central Committee then began to send official delegations to Bulgaria in the 1970s.[146]

The 1970s, however, were some of MPO's most turbulent years. In addition to decreasing membership and decreasing funds, there was severe infighting between MPO leaders. The leaders disagreed in the direction MPO should be taking; and aside from MPO's presidency in the 1970s, which was held by Asparuh Isakov, the other Central Committee positions were constantly being refilled. Virginia Nizamoff Surso, the daughter of Christo Nizamoff, wrote that Isakov's "presidency during the 1970s was marred by fragmentation in many different arenas that demanded constant guidance." Isakov's wife stated that "he struggled very hard to keep the organization together" and "he tried very hard to preserve the bonds and make peace." She acknowledged that during this time, MPO did not accomplish much at the national and international levels.[147]

Indeed, there was so much turmoil and changeover in MPO's leadership that it was impossible to focus on these larger issues. While Isakov was president during the 1970s, the MPO witnessed dozens of different people fill lower positions, such as vice-president, secretary, treasurer, and adviser. For example:

Vice-Presidents throughout the 1970s included Boris Dvorchanes, Elia Fileff, Reverend Kraeff, Bob Evanoff, Blagoy Markoff, Ivan Lebamoff, Toma Uzunoff, Nicholas Melanoff and Clement Nicoloff. Advisors throughout this decade included Stoyan Mitseff, Georgi Zahrieff, Chris Alusheff, Anton Popov, Dimiter Popov, Nick Nicolof, Nicola Filipov, Boris Pargoff, Eugene Kraeff, Vassil Shamanduroff, and Boris Gosheff, to name a few.[148]

By the 1980s, however, the MPO began to stabilize. While its membership levels never recovered, it was back on track to working for its goals on the national and international level. Ivan Lebamoff was now president, and this period could rightfully be called the Lebamoff age.[149]

Close to Lebamoff were people like his brother, George, Chris Alusheff, Dorie Atzeff, Virginia Nizamoff, and others. Ivan, who had served as Fort Wayne's mayor in the 1970s, was well-respected in the MPO community and well connected in Indiana, and was thus able to drum up more activity and support from MPO members than had been displayed in the previous two decades.

At the 65th convention in 1986, Ivan initiated a change in MPO's flag to symbolize MPO's rejuvenated spirit. The flag originally had black on the top and red on the bottom to indicate that Macedonia was in a state of mourning (black symbolizes mourning in Macedonia and other Balkan cultures). Ivan, however, reversed the two colors to put red on top, which would indicate that the MPO was ready to go to war for Macedonia. Moreover, under his tenure, the MPO moved its headquarters to Fort Wayne from Indianapolis (as more Macedonians lived in Fort Wayne); put a woman on the Central Committee for first time; hired another woman to administer the MPO; began collecting artifacts and books for museum-library; and hired a librarian, among many other initiatives.[150]

The final chapter in this MPO era, however, coincided with the MPO's 1990 convention. This is when the notorious Ivan Mihajlov passed away. For the MPO – which had been financing Mihajlov's exile and life in Italy for several decades – Mihajlov's passing was treated with the same sort of sadness people generally reserve for parents or siblings.

On September 6, the MPO Central Committee issued a circular to branches and members, informing them of Mihajlov's death. In part, it read:

Dear Brothers and Sisters: 1. The news that our beloved Ivan Mihailoff, affectionately referred to as Chico Radko, died September 5, 1990, in Rome at the age of 94 has saddened each of us. 2. Since the tragic assassination of Todor Alexandroff in 1924, he led IMRO with courage and brilliance, bringing the Macedonian Question to the forefront in the world arena. 3. His death brings a proud chapter of our history to a conclusion. ... 6. All chapters of the Macedonian Patriotic Organization are urged to hold a panihida (memorial service) in memory of Ivan Mihailoff on October 14, 1990. 7. ... His love for our cause and our people should be an inspiration to all of us.[151]

For most ethnic Macedonians, who view Mihajlov as a pro-Bulgarian opportunist, as the main reason why the Macedonians could never completely unite and as the butcherer of the Macedonian Cause, his death was welcomed or simply ignored. However, Mihajlov's financiers spent many weeks mourning. Their words of sympathy and sadness were not understandable to most

Macedonians. To MPO, though, the death of this near-centenarian shook their bones.

Stoyan Boyadjieff wrote:

Macedonia has lost its greatest pillar of strength. I felt the same when I lost my father. The weight that Ivan Mihailoff carried now falls on our shoulders. We are just beginning to understand this, and it strengthens me and all Macedonian Bulgarians. We won't give up!

Reverend George Nicoloff of St. Clement Macedono-Bulgarian Orthodox Church in Detroit said:

I've known him since I was a student at the University of Sofia and a member of the student organization 'Vardar'...I respected him. I loved him. I want to extend my sympathy to all of our brothers and sisters who are working for the freedom of Macedonia.

Others were briefer but displayed just as much grief. Dita Atzeff said that "the Macedonian Liberation Movement has lost a great leader just at a time when it most needed him." Chris Alusheff said that he felt like he "lost a very close friend." George Lebamoff summarized: "I believe that European historians will judge him favorably. When we were teenagers, his name was a household word. He is the last of the original great revolutionaries. IMRO has closed the circle."[152]

Mihajlov's death would usher in a new MPO era. But would this new era see a more pro-Macedonian MPO, or would it continue on its pro-Bulgarian path? The older generations who had clung to a Bulgarian identity were leaving this world, and the younger generations identified more as only Macedonians and less as Bulgarians. Would they stick around to reorient the MPO? Or would they uphold their forefathers' convictions?

Part III: The Modern Era

FIVE
Support for the Republic of Macedonia

At the start of the last decade of the 20th century, MPO's political efforts focused on three issues that most Macedonians had consumed themselves with: 1) recognition of Macedonia's independence from Yugoslavia; 2) respect for Macedonia's territorial integrity as other former Yugoslavian republics were engulfed in war; and 3) preserving Macedonia's name as the Republic of Macedonia. For the MPO, Macedonia's independence was an ideal that it had desired for seven decades. That Macedonia was not unified was of little importance because now there was a 'Macedonia for the Macedonians'. That the Macedonians in Macedonia were mostly ethnic Macedonians did not immediately bother the MPO because, as we will see, they assumed there would be time enough for Macedonians to grow closer to the Bulgarians in the future.

The primary battle, however, was preserving Macedonia's name and stability.

In 1992, just a few months after Macedonia's independence, Dita Atzeff, MPO's secretary at the time, wrote an editorial about Greece's refusal to recognize Macedonia.

The Greek government's claim that the republic of Macedonia has no right to the name 'Macedonia' should not affect the recognition of this republic as a free and independent state...Never before 1913 in the history of the Balkan Peninsula did Greece ever control or rule the geographic and

83

political nation known to antiquity and to medieval and modern Europe as Macedonia...Greece has not told the truth. It is time to forget her protests concerning a republic that already has a legislated guarantee of existing borders. It is time to grant full diplomatic recognition to the republic of Macedonia.[153]

Ivan Lebamoff also wrote that Greece's protestations were "trivial and unjustified and should not be the basis for denial of recognition of the Republic of Macedonia." On behalf of the MPO, he appealed "to members of the European Community to recognize the Republic of Macedonia without denying it the use of its rightful name."[154]

The following year, Ivan petitioned President Clinton to give "unconditional diplomatic recognition" to the Republic of Macedonia. "Such recognition would be a potent U.S. action to insure peace in that region and establish cohesiveness which would lessen the chances of civil war in Macedonia. He further stated that "recognition would also send a powerful signal to our Western allies that the United States values those nations that enthusiastically support U.S. international policies." He cited Macedonia's help in enforcing the economic embargo against Serbia, which resulted in throwing the Macedonian people into poverty.[155]

At the 1993 MPO convention, the MPO passed a resolution calling for international recognition of Macedonia. It read:

Whereas, Welcoming recognition of its independence by the United Nations and many nations of the world;

Whereas, Welcoming the confidence and support shown by world governments towards this new free and democratic state;

Whereas, Welcoming the presence of the United Nations peacekeepers and 300 US troops, formerly assigned to NATO, as a vital deterrent to potential aggression and as a safeguard for peace and stability in the Balkans;

Whereas, Noting that through peaceful actions, the Republic of Macedonia has demonstrated an essential commitment to promoting confidence and stability in the region, to fostering good relations with its neighbors, and to cooperating in economic and social matters;

Whereas, Noting that the Constitution of the Republic of Macedonia guarantees the rights of national, ethnic, religious and linguistic minorities in the Republic of Macedonia;

Whereas, Noting that the Republic of Macedonia, the heartland of the Balkans, is an example of peace and harmony in the world;

Therefore, be it Resolved

That the MPO urges the recognition of the Republic of Macedonia by the international community, support for democratic reforms in progress and promotion of the development of a free market economy in the Republic of Macedonia.[156]

Similarly, at the MPO's 75th annual convention in Michigan in 1996, the MPO "unanimously voted to urge the government of Greece to rescind its policy regarding the Republic of Macedonia's use of its name." The resolution proclaimed:

WHEREAS, The government of Greece is a signatory of many human and civil rights accords negotiated in good faith by and between governments throughout the world;

WHEREAS, Greece is a member of international bodies including the United Nations, European Union and NATO, all of which endorse open borders, unrestricted emigration and free markets and commerce;

WHEREAS, The Greek government has refused entry at its borders to many emigrants;

WHEREAS, Greece's restrictive policies bar many emigrants from visiting relatives and inhibit opportunities to reunite families;

WHEREAS, Emigrants are often prohibited from establishing legal and business links in Greece;

WHEREAS, Freedom of movement, open borders and unrestricted commerce are essential elements of free and open societies;

Therefore be it RESOLVED, The MPO strongly urges the government of Greece to rescind its discriminatory policies allowing open borders so that friends and relatives can reunite; by allowing its people to leave and return at will and by encouraging the expansion of commercial links between it and the Republic of Macedonia.

Getting recognition for the Republic of Macedonia, of course, was only one issue on MPO's agenda. In 2001, ethnic Albanian extremists initiated a terrorist campaign and armed insurrection that had the potential to create a civil war in Macedonia. In June of 2001, an article appeared in the *Macedonian Tribune* that encouraged the U.S. to support Macedonia against the Albanian insurgency. The article stated:

It is essential to note that the Republic of Macedonia…has one of the most successful human and civil rights records in the Balkans…Macedonia has a centuries-long history of multi-ethnic cooperation among a host of ethnic groups that have resided in the region since Biblical times. … The government of the Republic of Macedonia has made every effort to create an atmosphere in which a multi-ethnic society can develop and prosper. It has addressed, and continues to work diligently to resolve, the challenges of establishing a multicultural society.[157]

Through the mid-2000s, MPO conventions passed several resolutions annually on several of these important issues. They frequently denounced Greece's intransigency toward Macedonia, encouraged support for Macedonia's integration into NATO and the EU; and asked for international recognition of Macedonia as the Republic of Macedonia.

In the early 2000s, Greek-Americans initiated a campaign convincing state legislatures to pass resolutions that declared Macedonian history and culture was 'Greek' and to demand Macedonia refrain from calling itself 'Macedonia'. In response, like many Macedonian groups and individuals, the MPO lobbied these governments and others not to pass the resolutions or to pass pro-Macedonia resolutions.

One MPO article described the situation as a "virus". The Tribune wrote:

Lawmakers in Illinois, California and Missouri have unwittingly signed resolutions proclaiming that Macedonians are Greek and have been so for 3000 years. The same resolution is being considered in New Hampshire and

Texas. Which state will be the next? Only the Greek lobby knows.

Never mind that states should be paying attention to their local needs. Greek lawmakers and lobbyists are pushing forth their agenda, expropriating the time legislatures should be spending on budget deficits, road repairs, schools, and the like. ...

This newspaper urges every Macedonian to join in the fight against Greek usurpation of our national birthright as Macedonians. Each Macedonian family needs to contact its elected state officials and urge them not to unwittingly fall prey to the devious tactics of the Greek lobby's campaign of disinformation.[158]

And on March 9, 2004, Chris Evanoff, MPO president, wrote a letter to President Bush asking him to recognize the Republic of Macedonia. "I respectfully request that the United States of America formally recognize the Republic of Macedonia by its constitutional name," he wrote, "as determined by its citizens and elected leaders." Evanoff cited Macedonia's support for the U.S. during the Kosovo War, Macedonia's resolve to "faithfully" implement the Ohrid Framework Agreement (an agreement signed between ethnic Macedonian and ethnic Albanian politicians in Macedonia to end Albanian extremism in Macedonia), and Macedonia's "avowed" support for the U.S. War on terrorism.[159]

These issues preoccupied the MPO leadership and the MPO base. Clearly, their momentum was recharged by Macedonia's independence. Moreover, on the surface, it seemed as if the MPO had finally turned the corner: it seemed as if it had shaken off its Bulgarian leanings and was now embracing a pro-Macedonian agenda, including acceptance of the Macedonian ethnic identity.

However, beneath the surface, the MPO was harboring its same tendencies. There were pushes and pulls in many different directions, but a pro-Macedonian element did not successfully emerge.

SIX
Shifting Identities and Loyalties

George Lebamoff, who served on MPO's Central Committee in various positions in the 1990s and 2000s, recounted his views on identity in Macedonia. "I believe that if people feel they are truly Macedonian, good, but don't make me what I don't want to be."[160] This essentially represents MPO's most positive view on the ethnic Macedonian identity in the past three decades: there are people who identify as ethnic Macedonians, but MPO leaders do not identify as such.

George Lebamoff's understanding of the Macedonian identity is perhaps best highlighted when he explains discussions that his father would have with Macedonians:

My dad used to argue with younger people who would say they were not Bulgarians. "OK," he'd say, "The land is Macedonia, and has been from the time of Alexander the Great. Within Macedonia are seven different nationalities: the Greeks, the Serbs, the Gypsies, the Jews, the Turks, the Albanians, and the Bulgarians." He would point to one of his listeners, "Are you an Albanian?" "No." He'd ask about each of the other nationalities, and the answer would always be no. "Then you must be a Bulgarian." "No, I'm not Bulgarian. I'm Macedonian." Then he would try to explain again. "There is no Macedonian nationality, no Macedonian language. It's only the land. The language you speak is Bulgarian.[161]

Despite this staggering space between the MPO and other Macedonian groups on the issue of Macedonian ethnicity, Macedonia's independence created hope that MPO could work with other Macedonian groups and vice versa. In

December of 1991, MPO met with United Macedonian Organization (UMO) (a Canadian-Macedonian organization that formed shortly after the end of World War II) in Toronto.

The meeting began with the simple statement that both parties were not there to solve the differences that existed between them, but to strengthen areas in which they agreed. They discussed a common goal – a free and independent Macedonia. The result of this meeting was a resolution in which they demanded the international recognition of the Republic of Macedonia as an independent state.[162]

Nearly a year later, in September of 1992, the MPO sponsored a Forum on Macedonian Unity, which included leaders of MPO, UMO, and representatives of IMRO-DPMNE, Macedonia's right-wing and nationalist political party. The representatives signed a joint appeal to recognize the Republic of Macedonia.[163]

However, Pando Mladenov, an MPO leader in Toronto, protested vehemently to Ivan Lebamoff's meeting with the ethnic Macedonian groups. He wrote:

Has Ivan Lebamoff fallen into Serboslavia's communist trap? The United Macedonians are misguided political junkies, created by the Security Services of Serboslavia specifically to fight MPO. Its first President and organizer Christopher Zavella was sent to Skopje and afterwards trained for three years in the HQ of UDBA from where he managed to escape and ended up in Sofia. The officers and members of the United Macedonians were handpicked traitors infiltrated and controlled by the generals and colonels of UDBA directly from Belgrade. Good luck Ivan! Maybe you will learn a thing or two after you meet the families of the 25,000 Bulgarians killed by the Serbocommunists and the 200,000 that passed through

jails and the concentration camps in Idrizovo and Goli Otok?![164]

Putting aside the validity of Mladenov's claims, this move by Lebamoff created another significant divide in MPO. This rift culminated in 1994 when the MPO Toronto chapters, 'Victory' and 'Luben Dimitroff', led by Ivan Kardjov and George Mladenov (brother of Pando), refused to accept Macedonia as a separate nation even if Bulgarian could potentially become the official language. The MPO Central Committee in Indiana, however, could not accept this. MPO's motto had always been 'Macedonia for the Macedonians'; and while the MPO acknowledged that it would be desirable if Bulgarian could be the official language, they were adamant in their support for a separate Macedonian state and the term Macedonian being used as a 'civic identifier'. Moreover, the Toronto chapters were upset that the *Macedonian Tribune* began accepting articles written in Macedonian in addition to English and Bulgarian. Mladenov stated: "The Serbomans conquered the MPO from the inside like a Trojan horse." The Toronto 'Luben Dimitroff' chapter was thus expelled in 1994.[165]

Despite this decisive pro-Macedonia decision taken by MPO's Central Committee, it did not mean that MPO had shifted to a pro-Macedonian policy. At the 1993 convention in Toronto, Ivan Lebamoff stated that "Bulgaria and Macedonia were two countries with the same people" and he also "denied the existence of a separate Macedonian language, nation, and church."[166] Clearly, 'Macedonia for the Macedonians' did not mean ethnic Macedonians.

Guests at the 1993 convention, which was MPO's 72nd one and the 100-year anniversary of the establishment of IMRO, contained a stellar cast of prominent individuals from

Bulgaria as well as Macedonia. These included: Dr. Tatarcheff of Sofia, the nephew of Hristo Tatarcheff, first president of IMRO; Maria Koeva, daughter of Todor Aleksandrov; Elena Gyurkova, grandniece of Yordan Gyurkov, governor of Pirin Macedonia and chief lieutenant to Ivan Mihajlov; Veselin Evtimov, son of Simeon Evtimov, chief theorist for IMRO in the 1920s; Raina Drangova, daughter of Kiril Drangov, former chief of staff to Ivan Mihajlov; Ivan Shalev, son of Dimitar Shalev, who was mayor of Skopje in 1928; Stoyan Boyadjieff, president of IMRO-UMB in Sofia; Professor Dimitar Galev of Strumica who was president of the Agrarian Party of Macedonia; Vlado Perev, a radio journalist in Skopje; Ivan Grigorov, the chief justice of Bulgaria's Supreme Court; Simeon Simov, a journalist from Skopje; Ivan Katzarski, a professor from Skopje; Slavcho Kisselinchev, nephew of Lazar Kisselincheff, who led IMRO in Solun during Ilinden and was an early MPO leader; Christo Petsev, a lawyer in Strumica; Krum Chushkov, an IMRO activist in Veles; and Christo Matov, son of Christo Matov of Struga and chief theorist of IMRO.[167]

Risto Petsev, from Macedonia, was asked to speak and he announced his support for the MPO and the *Macedonian Tribune*:

I am a Macedonian patriot. I come by this honestly and naturally. My uncle...was brutally murdered by the Serbo-Communist UDBA in Macedonia in 1951. I am proud to be in Canada celebrating the 100th anniversary of the founding of IMRO and commemorating the 90th anniversary of Ilinden. ...

I am overwhelmed to be a part of an MPO convention, particularly one as monumental as this one. I am amazed at the work which the MPO and the *Macedonian Tribune* have

94

done since their founding. I am amazed at the significant contribution which the MPO has made in the last two years for the recognition of the Republic of Macedonia. Without your continued support and without the support of the MPO and the *Macedonian Tribune*, Macedonia would not be free, independent and recognized today. Recognition by the United Nations and most of the European Community can be attributed to the campaign exerted on world leadership by the MPO and the *Macedonian Tribune*. I spent several days in Fort Wayne, Indiana, and much time with the MPO and *Macedonian Tribune* staff. I was gratified to see your museum. I was inspired by your Monument to Freedom.

In the Republic of Macedonia, the MPO has been and will be a beacon of hope and fortification. We knew that as long as the MPO existed and continued to fight for the freedom of Macedonia, our goal would be achieved and our people would be free. Things in Macedonia are not easy. The old regime has merely changed its name. There is a great deal of pressure on us from Serbia and Greece. The economy is rough and living is not easy. But the people of Macedonia have hope. We know that in the end, we will win and that our long struggle will lead us to victory.[168]

This convention was one of the most elaborate ones that MPO had hosted in several decades. They spent a lot of money on flying in guests. While there were no official Macedonian representatives at the 1993 convention, there was an attempt to make connections between Macedonians and Bulgarians to expedite the MPO's dream of bringing Macedonians closer to Bulgarians.

And the MPO tried. At the 1996 convention, someone in the MPO sold copies of a booklet that was protesting "the inclusion of Macedonians as a separate ethnic group in the *Harvard Encyclopedia of American Ethnic Groups*." Many Macedonians were upset by MPO's insistence to not only declare that MPO was not an ethnic Macedonian organization, but by their attempt to persuade others to deny the existence of ethnic Macedonians. In the end, the MPO was not capable of preventing the publication of the *Harvard Encyclopedia* with ethnic Macedonians listed as a distinct group.[169]

With Chris Evanoff at the helm of MPO starting in late 1996, the MPO began reaching out to Macedonia's official representatives (in addition to Bulgarian politicians) to have more of an impact on official Macedonian policy. The 1997 convention was the first year that an ambassador of the Republic of Macedonia had ever attended an MPO convention.[170] In 1999, Macedonian Prime Minister Ljubco Georgievski attended and spoke to the assembled delegates,[171] and in 2008 Macedonian Ambassador Jolevski was given the MPO stage, as well.[172]

At the 2002 convention, Macedonian Ambassador to the U.S., Nikola Dimitrov, gave a convention address in which he praised the MPO and urged them to look forward:

It is my pleasure and honor to greet you on the occasion of the 81st Convention of the Macedonian Patriotic Organization – an organization with such a long and important tradition in promoting the truth about Macedonia. I salute the ongoing efforts of this organization in promoting Macedonian interests and values in this great country – the United States of America. Our country, the Republic of Macedonia, has a very long and rich history, and we are right in being proud to be Macedonians. The history is tragic because it is comprised of immense pain and injustice.

However, this history is also heroic by reason of the great determination of the Macedonians to persist. Yet, this does not mean that your organization should live in our history.

The Republic of Macedonia, a country born as a result of the sacred Ilinden tradition, has been facing its biggest challenge since independence. Therefore, I believe that those of us who love Macedonia and its tradition should focus on the present and on the future.

In these difficult and challenging times in our country's history we must all stand united, strong, and determined to protect what so many generations before us had only dreamt of – a free and independent Macedonia. We must follow the good example of this fine organization and as good Macedonians be truly patriotic and well organized.[173]

Moreover, at this 81st convention, the MPO had invited Bulgarian Ambassador Elena Poptodorova. She struck a more open and familial tone compared to Ambassador Dimitrov:

I do believe my presence here to be both a professional and a personal privilege. So thank you very much President Evanoff for extending this invitation...I'm also here to pay the respects of the Bulgarian people, of Bulgaria as a country and of the Bulgarian government...My country, Bulgaria, has always supported since the Declaration of Independence of Macedonia, its sovereignty, total integrity and well-being, and this has been a matter of conscious policy.

Being Macedonians, as you are, you would know that consensus is not the easiest thing to achieve in our part of the world; but, I have to say that one of the few issues in which the Bulgarian Parliament, the Bulgarian governments – in the plural – have had, throughout the years in those last 12 years, was our support for Macedonia...I was one of those who voted with this very hand the parliamentary decision for recognizing officially the Republic of Macedonia. ...

You would permit me a personal bias here by mentioning my excellent relationship with Ambassador Dimitrov, and it's really a pleasure to work with him and his team in Washington.[174]

This inching toward Macedonia's officials, however, did not mean MPO was inching away from a pro-Bulgarian philosophy. In late 1998, as president of the MPO, Evanoff sent a letter to Spas Tashev, a Bulgarian politician in charge of Bulgaria's right-wing IMRO political party, thanking him for his appearance at the 1998 convention. Evanoff wrote:

In behalf of the Central Committee of the Macedonian Patriotic Organization, I want to thank you and IMRO for the generous gifts including the bust of Ivan Mihailoff, the books, videos and cassettes which you gave me at the convention. They are a wonderful addition to the MPO library. Additionally, your generous donation will be acknowledged in our 70 year book. Please extend our warm greetings to Krasimir Karakachanov and the entire executive committee of the organization. I believe our two organizations have a lot in common and your attendance has officially opened the doors for us to work together. Based on our conversation, I am truly looking forward to working on the project which we discussed. I will be in touch with you soon so that we can begin to lay the groundwork for the project.[175]

It is worthwhile to note that Krasimir Karakachanov does not accept the existence of an ethnic Macedonian identity.

Further, at the 1999 MPO convention, Reverend Nedekoff, a Bulgarian priest in North America, emphasized the Bulgarian character of Macedonians. He said:

MPO was established by our fathers and forefathers, primarily by Bulgarians from Aegean Macedonia conceived the idea that we must keep and preserve our Bulgarian spirit. What we have heard yesterday, certain remarks from our visitors, bothered me. People from Macedonia, which is now

established as republic, have a right to associate. It is our sacred duty as Christians and as co-patriots to help the needy and the orphans in Macedonia; even the government to become more democratic. But, the expression, "*Macedonian Tribune* must cast aside the old propaganda; that we should change our alphabet; that we have to change?!" We don't have to change anything!

Before these people realized that they were slaves in Yugoslavia and Southern Serbia, the MPO members here in the US and Canada were fighting for their freedom, for the establishment of a free and independent Macedonia.

I've seen them stretching out their hands, asking for political, democratic, economic help, and the they want us to change to please them. Never! It will be sin before God, and before the memories of those who have given us the mineral water, the torch. We could help Macedonia and we should, but our organization is for us and those who believe as we do.[176]

In 2000, George Lebamoff reiterated the ideology that Macedonians were not an ethnic group. He told a Macedonian journalist that 'Macedonian' was a civic and not ethnic identity. "All people in Macedonia are Macedonians, because they are Macedonian citizens and have Macedonian passports, but by ethnicity they are Bulgarians, Albanians, Turks, etc."[177] Despite the reality that millions of people now identified as ethnic Macedonians, the MPO still alleged that no ethnic Macedonians exist.

Evanoff realized that the MPO was losing steam and credibility with such blatantly public anti-Macedonian viewpoints. He rebuked the accusation that MPO was a Bulgarian organization by stating that George Lebamoff was not authorized to officially speak for the MPO:

99

Since its inception, the MPO has never been a Bulgarian organization nor does it support unification of Macedonia with the Republic of Bulgaria or with any other state in the Balkans. The MPO Central Committee, through its elected President Chris Evanoff, is the only duly-authorized spokesperson for the organization. Mr. Lebamoff is neither a spokesperson for MPO nor a member of its governing board. Any comments attributed to him should not be construed as being representative of the organization or of its members.[178]

However, despite Evanoff's claim that the MPO was not a pro-Bulgarian organization, he did not acknowledge, in that letter, the existence of ethnic Macedonians or that MPO was an ethnic Macedonian organization. MPO fairly established that it did not support Macedonia's union with Bulgaria when it evicted MPO 'Luben Dimitroff' from MPO. But it still had not accepted, officially or publicly, the ethnic Macedonian identity.

Evanoff's tenure expired in 2006 and George Lebamoff was elected president. At the 2006 convention, Evanoff reflected on his success as head of MPO for a decade. He also appealed to MPO members to accept certain new realities:

But, today's MPO is comprised of members whose life experiences, interests, worldviews and expectations are vastly different than prior generations of MPO patriots. It is vitally important to recognize our evolution as an organization and adapt to its new membership realities in a constructive and appropriate way. I believe we have begun that process over the past ten years, and in my view, that is a measure of MPO progress. ...

The MPO, throughout the 20th century was the one constant -- the strongest voice that NEVER gave up the dream of an independent Macedonia. Not the Europeans, not the United

100

Nations, not the US and Canada and not even some Macedonians themselves remained true to the ideal. The MPO was always there, and it never wavered. And look at what was accomplished in 1991 with the formation of an independent Macedonian state. That, my friends, is among our greatest achievements as an organization. It is not perfection, but it is truly progress by every rational measure.

Our annual convention has hosted heads of state, ambassadors and key leaders of the Macedonian Republic and other Balkan countries. The opening address to this delegates meeting was provided by the US Ambassador to the Republic of Macedonia, The Honorable Gillian Milovanovic, and the keynote address at the banquet on Sunday evening will be delivered by The Honorable Ljupco Jordanovski, Macedonia's ambassador to the US. The MPO is acknowledged by them as a vital link between citizens and officials in the Republic and Macedonians living throughout North America. That, too, is progress.

The MPO has been, and continues to be, at the forefront in protecting and preserving our heritage and history as captured in the book *Macedonian Tribune Page One: Major Events of the 20th Century*, published by the organization in 1999. The project was led by Lou Todorov. In addition, our rights as an ethnic group have been defended through the efforts of MPO chapters in California, Illinois, Michigan and elsewhere that have withstood the onslaught of Greek lobbyists who sought to undermine what is rightfully ours ... our history and identity as a people. Resolutions passed in these states resulted from the collective efforts of our people to stand strong in the face of organized opposition and huge odds. We all succeeded when we stood and worked together -- that is progress!

Just a few years ago, the *Tribune* was published and distributed, for the first time, in the Republic. The special edition of the *Tribune* heralded the MPO's efforts to preserve our heritage when the resolutions that I just spoke of were passed in California, Illinois and Michigan. A generation ago, a Macedonian citizen could have been arrested for even possessing a copy of the *Tribune*. If you understand domestic Macedonian politics and the country's historic political aversion to the MPO, the publication of the *Tribune* in Skopje is an achievement of historic dimensions -- and yes, that, too, is progress.[179]

But MPO's direction did not shift away from a Bulgarian identity or heritage. In a *Macedonian Tribune* article in 2010, Larry Koroloff wrote about the history of Macedonia: "These two states [Greece and Serbia] proceeded to close all our Bulgarian schools and churches, and many of our intellectuals – teachers and clergy – were murdered." He wrote about how hundreds of Macedonian civilians were arrested in Vardar Macedonia "because they refused to deny their Bulgarian ethnicity." He concluded by appealing for a Macedonia according to MPO's consistent and true ideals: "The MPO believes that an ideal solution of the Macedonian Problem would be a free and united Macedonia where all ethnicities – Bulgarian, Albanian, Vlach and others would enjoy equal rights."[180]

Despite these numerous and obvious pro-Bulgarian sentiments of the MPO, in 2009 and 2010, the United Macedonian Diaspora (a Macedonian-American group that sprouted in 2003) decided to join the MPO in a coalition seeking to encourage Macedonian-Americans to declare their Macedonian ethnicity in the U.S. Census.

Many community leaders warned UMD not to involve itself with MPO. Dusan Sinadinoski, founder and first elected president of St. Mary's Macedonian Orthodox Church in Michigan, wrote an open letter criticizing UMD's decision. In part, he wrote:

First, despite the good intentions of the Macedonian diaspora, it is unacceptable for UMD to enter into this coalition because the composition of the coalition in no way can be considered a legitimate and representative body of the Macedonian diaspora. The problem is that the composition of the 'Macedonian' Census Coalition includes several organizations that are suspicious of the Macedonian identity or who openly deny the Macedonian identity. As an example, this coalition includes the Macedonian Patriotic Organization (MPO). ...

The assumption of the coalition is that Macedonians in America would enjoy more benefits and privileges if they prove that their number is larger than thought. This is speculative in nature and does not reflect the actual social picture in America. But to have any noticeable benefit, UMD should not enter into a coalition with the MPO and thus allow it to represent the Macedonian diaspora. UMD should know that this proven anti-Macedonian organization continues to deny the Macedonian ethnic identity, even though Macedonia is an independent state. Since the formation of the MPO, and until today, the Macedonian Diaspora in America and Canada was continuously and systematically destroyed by this organization. MPO as then and now calls the Macedonians Bulgarian-Macedonians and denies the existence of ethnic Macedonians. For the MPO, the adjective "Macedonian" is a geographical qualifier and does not imply a particular ethnic nation.[181]

Sinadinoski and others were right to warn against joining in such a coalition. MPO's leaders soon suggested that Macedonians should classify themselves as Macedono-Bulgarians on the U.S. Census.

As a result, UMD removed MPO from its census coalition in February of 2010. In a statement, UMD president Metodija

Koloski said that UMD's "efforts to form the coalition so that several Macedonian-American groups could work for a common cause – an accurate count of Macedonian-Americans" was jeopardized when "the MPO deviated from that goal by calling on its members to identify themselves as something other than Macedonian on U.S. Census forms." Koloski added that "the Coalition determined that the MPO should no longer be included in the Coalition which is continuing its efforts to educate Macedonian-Americans of the importance of participating in the Census and to respond in a consistent manner to questions relating to race, ethnicity and national origin."[182]

Fred Meanchoff, as MPO's treasurer, wrote an article in the Macedonian Tribune in May of 2010 explaining and clarifying his and MPO's position on the Census campaign:

Today I would like to comment on the word ethnic, a word that has been erroneously interchanged with nationality to the detriment of the unity of the Macedonian Cause. During the 2010 American census count, a movement was afoot to write in the word Macedonian under the question of ethnicity...Nick Stefanoff and I were challenged by a group on Facebook called 'Support for the United Diaspora for the Census in America' for our supposed anti-Macedonian stance concerning the write-in campaign.

NO! THIS IS NOT TRUE. We wanted to ensure that the ideals of a 'free and independent Macedonia', a Switzerland of the Balkans, were kept alive and not thwarted by those agencies set to destroy what the Macedonian Patriotic Organization champions. Nick and I were called traitors and Bulgarian nationalists. On the contrary, we uphold beliefs that are true and just, ideals based on an intense history of truths and not naïve principles lost in a haze of altered post World War II pro-Yugoslav propaganda. ...

My parents were Bulgarians from Macedonia, but they were Macedonian patriots first and foremost...The origin of my parent's speech was Bulgarian...Our ethnicity cannot be linked to just 'Macedonian'. It must be expressed truly as Bulgarian, Greek, Aroumanian, Albanian and the rest of Macedonia's ethnic groups...The ethnic issue of the Macedonian-Bulgarian is of importance and stature within the recording of statistics.[183]

At the 2012 MPO Convention, Fred Meanchoff (now president of MPO) reiterated his stance on MPO's ideals and ethnic identity. He said: "I strongly believe in the idea of a free and independent Macedonia, a Switzerland of the Balkans, composed of Greeks, Bulgarians, Aromanians, Jews, Muslims – anyone born within the natural geographic boundaries of Macedonia." He insisted that MPO was "an organization...founded by the Bulgarian immigrants who came from the old country." In the end, of course, he insisted that he was "very proud to be a Macedonian."[184]

At this convention, however, Ljubomir Todorov appeared to be more accommodating of the ethnic Macedonian identity. He said that a Macedonian was "a person of any ethnic background who was born in the geographic region of Macedonia or whose origins are from the geographic region of Macedonia." Per usual, he insisted that "the term Macedonian represents all the people of Macedonia regardless of their ethnic or religious origins." But he noted that the MPO was "neither an ethnic Macedonian nor an ethnic Bulgarian organization. It's a patriotic organization of all the people from Macedonia whose ideal is a free, independent and united Macedonia." He then said that if Macedonians wanted to find relatives, they just have to "travel to Bulgaria, where there are more than 1 million people who can trace their origins to Macedonia."[185]

Todorov insisted that MPO was not an ethnic Macedonian or ethnic Bulgarian organization.

However, this is the line that the MPO generally espoused publicly: the MPO is a civic organization for different ethnicities that hail from Macedonia. Yet, there still was no direct acknowledgement of the ethnic Macedonian identity, and it was proven that the MPO is incapable of shaking off its pro-Bulgarian tendencies.

Conclusion

MPO's future does not look promising. If it does not completely degenerate (there are only seven chapters remaining, down from about three dozen at MPO's peak), then it will likely become politically irrelevant. Several reasons support this assertion.

First, most ethnic Macedonians are neither interested in it nor aware of it. Other groups (social, cultural and political) unambiguously work for both the betterment of Macedonia and development of the ethnic Macedonian community. These groups are more desirable to ethnic Macedonians. Second, MPO's events tend to attract people who are third and fourth generation Macedonian-Americans. These Macedonians generally are removed from the political and identity battles and their interests are instead focused on cultural and social activities. Certainly, some recent Macedonian immigrants venture into MPO's orbit, usually out of historical ignorance or convenience, and this new membership and support is the only way MPO can realistically stay relevant. Still, most MPO leaders and members do not attend Macedonian Orthodox churches. This is significant because most ethnic Macedonians learn about, and engage in, social and cultural activities through these local church communities. MPO's repute in these communities is wanting.

Third, MPO never realized the type of 'Macedonia for the Macedonians' within its organization that it promoted and promotes for Macedonia; that is, MPO's membership primarily consisted (and consists) of those individuals who considered themselves ethnic Bulgarians, with some ethnic Macedonians and Aromanians involved. Very few people with roots in Macedonia that identify as Albanians, Turks, Greeks and Serbs have joined the organization. MPO sought to create a 'Switzerland of the Balkans', but the organization looked more like a microcosm of Bulgaria's chauvinistic dreams than a Switzerland or Macedonia. The MPO was, and is, predominantly an ethnic Bulgarian organization: its leaders can only fool themselves for so long.

However, whether or not MPO perseveres as a meaningful advocacy organization, those who espouse its pro-Bulgarian views still persist in their efforts and threaten the Macedonian Cause as established by the ethnic Macedonian community. If MPO exists, then there is always an avenue for Bulgaria and the Bulgarian chauvinists to reach the Macedonians and infiltrate the Macedonian Cause. If MPO disintegrates, then many of those within it may seek to infuse themselves and their ideologies into other Macedonian organizations.

In fact, this exodus from MPO to join other organizations has happened not infrequently. On one hand, there are those Macedonians who disassociated with the MPO because its ideologies (refusal to recognize the Macedonian ethnic identity and Macedonian language) contrasted with their personal convictions. On the other hand, there are MPO members who have left the MPO for other organizations without publicly accepting the Macedonian ethnic identity for themselves.

Some MPO leaders have found themselves engrained in the United Macedonian Diaspora's work. In addition to the ill-advised UMD census coalition with the MPO, UMD has worked closely with former MPO president Chris Evanoff, who even serves on UMD's Advisory Council.[186] There have also been other former MPO members involved with UMD, in one way or another.

This UMD acceptance of (and collaboration with) MPO extends back to the early months of UMD's formation. In August of 2004, UMD President Metodija Koloski encouraged Macedonians to work with MPO. He wrote that Macedonians should not be joining the MPO to "form a pro-Bulgarian national consciousness," but instead should join "to get rid of the pro-Bulgarian national consciousness" within the organization's ranks. He said, "I will never excuse what the past MPO has done, but we can work to help MPO do good from now on." Koloski also expressed confidence that the MPO would soon amend its bylaws to affirm that ethnic Macedonians do indeed exist. He insisted that he would succeed in helping MPO change their pro-Bulgarian mentality and that people should believe him when he said, "we can work with MPO."[187] Koloski underscored that "the good part about MPO is that it is changeable."[188] Since Koloski wrote these words fourteen years ago, the MPO's bylaws still do not acknowledge an ethnic Macedonian identity; UMD had to eject MPO from a project on which the two groups were collaborating; and the MPO still espouses pro-Bulgarian views.

Koloski further defended MPO's work in another message. He wrote:

Another confusion is the use of "Bulgarian" language in their newspaper, which I highly recommend subscribing to, very informative, no offense to anyone here. I'm subscribed to the *Tribune* because I want to learn what MPO does and also because it is in English and that is the language I was educated in. When my father and uncle had a meeting with

one of the MPO Board of Directors in the late 90s, which they call Central Committee...they asked him about the Bulgarian language use. The MPO director said that this language is the language they always spoke, and that it is a Macedonian language.

As far as conventions go...it is not that MPO holds their convention to spite our church convention. It is because MPO has held their convention since 1922 during Labor Day Weekend. Many Macedonians have asked MPO to change it or to work together with the church to make it at the same location together. MPO's response is this year is our 83rd convention, the church has their 30th, we will not alter our date or location because it has been a tradition. Just like how we know our convention is Labor Day Weekend, they know theirs is also. If anyone did anything to spite someone, it was the church's decision to hold their convention during the same weekend as the MPO one. I suggest a Church convention during Memorial Day Weekend, because having two conventions at the same time in the same place will be hectic.

Also for some of us that want to attend the MPO convention [we] cannot because the church convention is the same weekend. I have heard many people say they prefer to go to the MPO convention because there are not any damages to the hotels like at the church one. I do not blame them. ...

To see a list of all MPO conventions go to macedonian.org click on MPO and then MPO activities. Just because you attend an MPO event does not meant [sic] your [sic] a pro-Bulgarian. What about people who are Macedonian Orthodox but have family in MPO? My friend married an MPO member, and his family is soooooo pro-Macedonian working to get rid of the pro-Bulgarianism of the past MPO![189]

Aside from demonstrating Koloski's blatantly misguided understanding of the MPO, this message reveals, to a certain extent, how MPO has managed to legitimize itself in some ethnic Macedonians' eyes. It is worrying when ethnic Macedonian leaders, like Koloski, who are active in the Macedonian Cause, deem MPO to be a potential beneficial force promoting the Macedonian Cause. If Macedonian-American leaders are being duped and convinced by the MPO's sly double-speak, what kind of 'magic' can the MPO work on Macedonians who are removed from these issues and unfamiliar with MPO's troubled history?

Whether or not the MPO persists or disintegrates, its undeniable history will always serve as a reminder of that for which it truly stands: an independent Macedonia for the Macedono-Bulgarians. The MPO might be pro-Macedonia, but it is not a pro-Macedonian organization. Simply stated, we all must accept this uncomfortable truth and move on.

ENDNOTES

[1] Bylaws of the Macedonian Patriotic Organization of the United States and Canada, Article III, Section 9, state: "The terms "Macedonians" and "Macedonian immigrants" used in these bylaws pertain equally to all nationality groups in Macedonia—Bulgarians, Aroumanians, Turks, Albanians, and others. As used in these MPO Bylaws, these terms have only geographic and not ethnographic meaning."
http://macedonian.org/joomla/index.php?option=com_content&view=article&id=113&Itemid=93 . Last accessed October 13, 2018.

[2] The Pan-Macedonian Association has some similarities and differences to the MPO. They say they hail from geographical Macedonia and call themselves Macedonians, but they also claim they are ethnic Greeks. They don't recognize ethnic Macedonians or the Macedonian language. In this sense, you can substitute 'Greek' for 'Bulgarian' and the two groups sound similar. However, the MPO advocates for an independent Macedonia (and used to advocate for a United Macedonia), while the Pan-Macedonians believe that Macedonia belongs in Greece and that the Republic of Macedonia is not really Macedonia.

[3] In Re Incorporation: The Macedonian Political Organization of the United States of America and Canada, Indiana Secretary of State, July 6, 1925; Articles of Incorporation, The Indianapolis News (Indianapolis, Indiana), Jul 7, 1925, Page 28

[4] Periods before this are often confusing for many reasons and for all Balkan peoples. For example, Western observers generally wrote (in the 18th century) about all Balkan Orthodox Christians as 'Greeks', as they referred to the Orthodox religion as the Greek Christian religion. People's identities were given to them based on what others called their religion and even language. This does not mean that individuals didn't refer to themselves as Macedonian; but before this period, it is hard to always conclusively prove what someone meant when he said he was Macedonian, or what he meant when he said he was Greek, Bulgarian, Serbian, etc.

[5] Gunman Robs Store of $200, The Indianapolis Star (Indianapolis, Indiana) 05 Jan 1958, Page 7. The author also found three records of Theodore Vasiloff in www.familsearch.org database, two who were described as living in Montana during the 1920 census and one who was born in 1894 (making him around the same age as our Theodore Vasiloff) and having died in 1966 in California; however, they have not been conclusively linked to the Theodore Vasiloff in the MPO.

[6] Choir Will Aid Beech Grove Relief Fund, The Indianapolis Star (Indianapolis, Indiana) 09 Feb 1932, Page 10

[7] "Indiana Naturalization Records and Indexes, 1848-1992," database with images, FamilySearch (https://familysearch.org/ark:/61903/1:1:QVM8-4DV7 : 8 November 2017), Stanley Georgieff, 1928; citing Naturalization, Indianapolis,

Marion, Indiana, United States, NARA NAID 5682644, National Archives at Chicago, Illinois.

[8] "Indiana Naturalization Records and Indexes, 1848-1992," database with images, FamilySearch (https://familysearch.org/ark:/61903/1:1:QVM8-HSCX : 8 November 2017), Stanley Georgieff, 1929; citing Naturalization, Indianapolis, Marion, Indiana, United States, NARA NAID 5682644, National Archives at Chicago, Illinois.

[9] In Re Incorporation: The Macedonian Political Organization of the United States of America and Canada, Indiana Secretary of State, July 6, 1925

[10] "United States Census, 1930," database with images, FamilySearch (https://familysearch.org/ark:/61903/1:1:X4YX-BLG : accessed 11 October 2018), Gill Sarbinoff, Indianapolis, Marion, Indiana, United States; citing enumeration district (ED) ED 372, sheet 7A, line 4, family 131, NARA microfilm publication T626 (Washington D.C.: National Archives and Records Administration, 2002), roll 611; FHL microfilm 2,340,346.

[11] "Indiana Naturalization Records and Indexes, 1848-1992," database with images, FamilySearch (https://familysearch.org/ark:/61903/1:1:QVM8-HXNG : 8 November 2017), Gill Sarbinoff, 1930; citing Naturalization, Indianapolis, Marion, Indiana, United States, NARA NAID 5682644, National Archives at Chicago, Illinois.

[12] "Find A Grave Index," database, FamilySearch (https://familysearch.org/ark:/61903/1:1:QVKK-12YH : 13 December 2015), Gill Sarbinoff, ; Burial, Indianapolis, Marion, Indiana, United States of America, Crown Hill Cemetery; citing record ID 46008600, Find a Grave, http://www.findagrave.com.

[13] Gregory Michaelidis, Salvation Abroad: Macedonian Migration to North America and the Making of Modern Macedonia, 1870-1970, University of Maryland Ph.D. Dissertation, 2005, Pg. 151, 152.

[14] Јордан Чкатров, http://www.mn.mk/makedonski-legendi/10070-Jordan-Ckatrov . Last accessed October 11, 2018.

[15] Lubomir Todorov, MPO: 90 Years of Struggle for a Macedonian State, A Keynote speech delivered at the Grand Banquet of the 91st Annual MPO Convention in Fort Wayne, Indiana, September 2, 2012.

[16] Сребрен Поппетров, http://www.mn.mk/makedonski-legendi/13156 . Last accessed October 11, 2018.

[17] See Victor Sinadinoski, Macedonians in America: Their Lives and Struggles in the 21st century, 2017.

[18] Lubomir Todorov, MPO: 90 Years of Struggle for a Macedonian State, A Keynote speech delivered at the Grand Banquet of the 91st Annual MPO Convention in Fort Wayne, Indiana, September 2, 2012.

[19] Lubomir Todorov, MPO: 90 Years of Struggle for a Macedonian State, A Keynote speech delivered at the Grand Banquet of the 91st Annual MPO Convention in Fort Wayne, Indiana, September 2, 2012.

[20] Will Give Show, Harrisburg Telegraph (Harrisburg, Pennsylvania) 18 Jan 1922, Page 8

[21] Forward Plea for Macedonia, Harrisburg Telegraph (Harrisburg, Pennsylvania) 22 Jul 1922, Sat Page 18

[22] See Victor Sinadinoski, David Nakoff: Leader of Steelton's Macedonians and Founder of the First Macedonian-American Orthodox Church, 2018.

[23] Lubomir Todorov, MPO: 90 Years of Struggle for a Macedonian State, A Keynote speech delivered at the Grand Banquet of the 91st Annual MPO Convention in Fort Wayne, Indiana, September 2, 2012.

[24] Lubomir Todorov, MPO: 90 Years of Struggle for a Macedonian State, A Keynote speech delivered at the Grand Banquet of the 91st Annual MPO Convention in Fort Wayne, Indiana, September 2, 2012.

[25] "United States Census, 1920," database with images, FamilySearch (https://familysearch.org/ark:/61903/1:1:MZWR-8MJ : accessed 12 October 2018), Simon Balkoff in household of Edward F Herbst, Detroit Ward 16, Wayne, Michigan, United States; citing ED 494, sheet 9B, line 58, family 196, NARA microfilm publication T625 (Washington D.C.: National Archives and Records Administration, 1992), roll 815; FHL microfilm 1,820,815.

[26] "United States Census, 1930," database with images, FamilySearch (https://familysearch.org/ark:/61903/1:1:X79D-FK4 : accessed 12 October 2018), Andrea Kostoff, Detroit (Districts 0251-0500), Wayne, Michigan, United States; citing enumeration district (ED) ED 289, sheet 18A, line 9, family 21, NARA microfilm publication T626 (Washington D.C.: National Archives and Records Administration, 2002), roll 1043; FHL microfilm 2,340,778.

[27] "Vermont, St. Albans Canadian Border Crossings, 1895-1954," database with images, FamilySearch (https://familysearch.org/ark:/61903/1:1:QKQM-2RNT : 16 March 2018), Lambro Nicoloff, 1895-1924; citing M1461, Soundex Index to Canadian Border Entries through the St. Albans, Vermont, District, 1895-1924, 285, NARA microfilm publications M1461, M1463, M1464, and M1465 (Washington D.C.: National Archives and Records Administration, publication year); FHL microfilm 1,473,085.

[28] "United States Border Crossings from Canada to United States, 1895-1956," database, FamilySearch (https://familysearch.org/ark:/61903/1:1:XL17-KMV : 27 November 2014), Lambro Nicoloff, Nov 1909; from "Border Crossings: From Canada to U.S., 1895-1954," database and images, Ancestry (http://www.ancestry.com : 2010); citing Ship , arrival port Port Huron, Michigan,, line 1, NARA microfilm publication M1464, Records of the Immigration and Naturalization Service, RG 85, (Washington D.C.: National Archives and Records Administration, n.d.), roll 111.

[29] "United States World War II Draft Registration Cards, 1942," database with images, FamilySearch (https://familysearch.org/ark:/61903/1:1:J4SK-DZ8 : 8 November 2017), Christo Spiroff, 1942; citing NARA microfilm publication

M1936, M1937, M1939, M1951, M1962, M1964, M1986, M2090, and M2097 (Washington D.C.: National Archives and Records Administration, n.d.).

[30] Македонските българи са ядрото на Българщината зад Океана, http://freemacedonia.net/statia.php?sn=449&t=7& . Last accessed October 11, 2018.

[31] Сребрен Поппетров, http://www.mn.mk/makedonski-legendi/13156 . Last accessed October 11, 2018.

[32] Lubomir Todorov, MPO: 90 Years of Struggle for a Macedonian State, A Keynote speech delivered at the Grand Banquet of the 91st Annual MPO Convention in Fort Wayne, Indiana, September 2, 2012.

[33] Coordinating Committee of the Youth Sections With the Macedonian Patriotic Organizations of the United States and Canada, Macedonians in North America, Toronto, 1960, Pg. 7.

[34] Lubomir Todorov, MPO: 90 Years of Struggle for a Macedonian State, A Keynote speech delivered at the Grand Banquet of the 91st Annual MPO Convention in Fort Wayne, Indiana, September 2, 2012.

[35] MPO History, http://macedonian.org/joomla/index.php?option=com_content&view=article&id=49&Itemid=58 . Last accessed October 10, 2018.

[36] Christo Nizamoff, Popoff Leads MPO During Greek Civil War, Macedonian Tribune, Nov. 8, 1984, http://www.macedonian.org/about/history_popoff.asp . Last accessed October 12, 2018.

[37] Lubomir Todorov, MPO: 90 Years of Struggle for a Macedonian State, A Keynote speech delivered at the Grand Banquet of the 91st Annual MPO Convention in Fort Wayne, Indiana, September 2, 2012.

[38] Christo Nizamoff, Popoff Leads MPO During Greek Civil War, Macedonian Tribune, Nov. 8, 1984, http://www.macedonian.org/about/history_popoff.asp . Last accessed October 12, 2018.

[39] http://www.wikiwand.com/bg/Потребител_беседа:Drenowe , Citing Makedonski Almanah, 1940, Pg. 223, 345; The Lebamoff Family Home Page; https://www.genealogy.com/ftm/l/e/b/Thomas-G-Lebamoff/index.html . Last accessed October 12, 2018.

[40] Central Committee of Trustees, 2018-2019, http://www.macedonian.org/joomla/index.php?option=com_content&view=article&id=48 . Last accessed October 12, 2018.

[41] Лазар Киселинчев, http://dictionnaire.sensagent.leparisien.fr/%D0%9B%D0%B0%D0%B7%D0%B0%D1%80%20%D0%9A%D0%B8%D1%81%D0%B5%D0%BB%D0%B8%D0%BD%D1%87%D0%B5%D0%B2/bg-bg/ . Last Accessed October 13, 2018.

[42] Dimitar Ljorovski Vamvakovski, The Arrest and Prosecution of Komitadji in Greece at the Beginning of the 20th Century, ed. Australian Macedonian Human Rights Committee, The Macedonian Human Rights Review, Iss. 27, July 2017.

[43] Лазар Киселинчев, http://mn.mk/makedonski-legendi/13930-Lazar-Kiselincev . Last accessed October 13, 2018.

[44] Лазар Киселинчев, http://dictionnaire.sensagent.leparisien.fr/%D0%9B%D0%B0%D0%B7%D0%B0%D1%80%20%D0%9A%D0%B8%D1%81%D0%B5%D0%BB%D0%B8%D0%BD%D1%87%D0%B5%D0%B2/bg-bg/ . Last Accessed October 13, 2018.

[45] Christo Nizamoff, Struggle for Freedom: Reflections and Reminiscences, Hoosier Press, Indianapolis, 1985, Pg. 100.

[46] Christo Nizamoff, Struggle for Freedom: Reflections and Reminiscences, Hoosier Press, Indianapolis, 1985, Pg. 101.

[47] Christo Nizamoff, Struggle for Freedom: Reflections and Reminiscences, Hoosier Press, Indianapolis, 1985, Pg. 105.

[48] Christo Nizamoff, Struggle for Freedom: Reflections and Reminiscences, Hoosier Press, Indianapolis, 1985, Pg. 106.

[49] Lubomir Todorov, MPO: 90 Years of Struggle for a Macedonian State, A Keynote speech delivered at the Grand Banquet of the 91st Annual MPO Convention in Fort Wayne, Indiana, September 2, 2012.

[50] Christo Nizamoff, Struggle for Freedom: Reflections and Reminiscences, Hoosier Press, Indianapolis, 1985, Pg. 127, 128.

[51] Macedonian Tribune Past Editors, http://macedonian.org/joomla/index.php?option=com_content&view=article&id=52&Itemid=62 . Last accessed October 4, 2018.

[52] Christo Nizamoff, Struggle for Freedom: Reflections and Reminiscences, Hoosier Press, Indianapolis, 1985, Pg. 128.

[53] See generally Joseph Swire, Bulgarian Conspiracy, 1939 for a more detailed recount and analysis of the IMRO's split.

[54] Macedonian Tribune Past Editors, http://macedonian.org/joomla/index.php?option=com_content&view=article&id=52&Itemid=62 . Last accessed October 4, 2018.

[55] Premier to King Without Kingdom, Lansing State Journal (Lansing, Michigan), Dec 10, 1931, Page 5

[56] Macedonian Tribune Past Editors, http://macedonian.org/joomla/index.php?option=com_content&view=article&id=52&Itemid=62 . Last accessed October 4, 2018.

[57] Christo Nizamoff, Struggle for Freedom: Reflections and Reminiscences, Hoosier Press, Indianapolis, 1985, Pg. 129.

[58] Macedonian Tribune Past Editors, http://macedonian.org/joomla/index.php?option=com_content&view=article&id=52&Itemid=62 . Last accessed October 4, 2018.

[59] Boris Zografoff, Macedonia in Fighting Mood,   The Indianapolis Star (Indianapolis, Indiana) 09 May 1929, Page 8

[60] Macedonian Tribune Past Editors,
http://macedonian.org/joomla/index.php?option=com_content&view=article&id=52&Itemid=62 . Last accessed October 4, 2018.
[61] Trendafil Mitev, MPO in the United States, Canada and Australia.
[62] Christo Nizamoff, Struggle for Freedom: Reflections and Reminiscences, Hoosier Press, Indianapolis, 1985, Pg. 129.
[63] Christo Nizamoff, MPO Grows in Stature Under Pandil G. Shaneff,
https://web.archive.org/web/19971014012707/http://www.macedonian.org:80/ . Last Accessed October 11, 2018.

[64] Boris Zografoff, Good Will Toward All, The Indianapolis Star (Indianapolis, Indiana) 27 Sep 1930, Page 10
[65] Lubomir Todorov, MPO: 90 Years of Struggle for a Macedonian State, A Keynote speech delivered at the Grand Banquet of the 91st Annual MPO Convention in Fort Wayne, Indiana, September 2, 2012.
[66] Macedonian Tribune Past Editors,
http://macedonian.org/joomla/index.php?option=com_content&view=article&id=52&Itemid=62 . Last accessed October 4, 2018.
[67] Trendafil Mitev, MPO in the United States, Canada and Australia.
[68] Hristo Kostov, Contested Ethnic Identity: The Case of Macedonian Canadians in Toronto, 1940-1996, Ph.D. Thesis, Department of History, University of Ottawa, 2009, Pg. 171.
[69] Background Whereabouts and Activities of Ivan Mihailov, 16 April 1953, Approved for release 1999/09/10, CIA-REDP83-00423R000300710001-9.
[70] Background, Whereabouts and Activities of Ivan Mihailov, 16 April 1953, Approved for release 1999/09/10, CIA-REDP83-00423R000300710001-9.
[71] Background, Whereabouts and Activities of Ivan Mihailov, 16 April 1953, Approved for release 1999/09/10, CIA-REDP83-00423R000300710001-9.
[72] Joseph S. Roucek, Balkan Politics: International Relations in No Man's Land, Stanford University Press, Stanford, 1948, Pg. 157.
[73] Macedonians In Political Battle, Calgary Herald (Calgary, Alberta, Canada), Sep 19, 1932, Page 2
[74] Macedonian Injustice, The Akron Beacon Journal (Akron, Ohio), Mar 5, 1934, Page 4
[75] Refutes Macedonia, The Akron Beacon Journal (Akron, Ohio), Mar 8, 1934, Page 4
[76] Arrest Communists at Fort Wayne, The Daily Reporter (Greenfield, Indiana), Sep 3, 1934, Page 4
[77] 2 Akronites are Honored At Macedonian Convention, The Akron Beacon Journal (Akron, Ohio), Sep 3, 1935, Page 24
[78] "Discusses Balkan Peace," The Indianapolis News (Indianapolis, Indiana) 04 Sep 1923, Page 12.

[79] "Macedonians Seek Treaty Revisions," *The Indianapolis Star* (Indianapolis, Indiana) 05 Nov 1923, Page 11

[80] P.G. Shaneff, Macedonia Wants Autonomy, The Indianapolis Star (Indianapolis, Indiana), Apr 20, 1928, Page 6

[81] Balkan Situation Still Menace, Says Speaker, The Indianapolis News (Indianapolis, Indiana), Jun 30, 1925, Page 18

[82] Plans Disucssed for Balkan Union, Aiding Macedonia, The Indianapolis Star (Indianapolis, Indiana), Sep 8, 1925, Page 5

[83] P. Shaneff and L.L. Kisselintcheff, Macedonians in Peril, The Indianapolis Star (Indianapolis, Indiana), Nov 6, 1925, Page 6

[84] Macedonians to Present Drama, News-Journal (Mansfield, Ohio), Feb 24, 1927, Page 20

[85] Macedonians to Celebrate Anniversary, News-Journal (Mansfield, Ohio) 20 Jul 1927, Page 16

[86] Macedonians Protest Against Property Sale, The Indianapolis Star (Indianapolis, Indiana), May 7, 1927, Page 7

[87] Macedonians Make Plea, The Gazette (Montreal, Quebec, Canada), Aug 12, 1927, Page 12

[88] George Popoff, Macedonian Troubles, Dayton Daily News (Dayton, Ohio), Oct 17, 1927, Page 6

[89] Macedonian Organization Sees Menace of European War in Balkan Situation, The Evening News (Harrisburg, Pennsylvania), Oct 22, 1927, Page 9

[90] P.G. Sirmin, Macedonian Loyalty, The Indianapolis Star (Indianapolis, Indiana), Dec 9, 1927, Page 6

[91] Balkan Embers Fanned Again, Detroit Free Press (Detroit, Michigan), Sep 10, 1928, Page 19

[92] The Evening News (Harrisburg, Pennsylvania), Oct 13, 1928

[93] Macedonian-Croatian Appeal, The Evening News (Harrisburg, Pennsylvania), Mar 19, 1929, Page 3

[94] Free Government Movement is Found Gaining in Balkans, The Indianapolis Star (Indianapolis, Indiana), Mar 31, 1929, Page 9

[95] Naum Bitsoff, The Situation in the Balkans, The Cincinnati Enquirer (Cincinnati, Ohio), Apr 28, 1930, Page 18

[96] League Resolutions Sent By Macedonians, The Evening News (Harrisburg, Pennsylvania), Nov 7, 1930, Page 2

[97] P.G. Shaneff, Help Don't Hinder, The Indianapolis Star (Indianapolis, Indiana), May 20, 1930, Page 8

[98] P.G. Shaneff, Defends the Bulgarians, The Indianapolis Star (Indianapolis, Indiana), Jul 17, 1930, Page 8

[99] Paul G. Sirmin, Another Macedonian Cry, The Indianapolis Star (Indianapolis, Indiana), Aug 13, 1932, Page 6

[100] The Persecuted Bulgars, The Atlanta Constitution (Atlanta, Georgia), Apr 8, 1933, Page 4

[101] Macedonians Protest to Bulgarian Monarch, The Indianapolis News (Indianapolis, Indiana), Jul 13, 1934, Page 5

[102] Subjugated Macedonians Ask Independent State, Detroit Free Press (Detroit, Michigan), Oct 7, 1934, Page 133

[103] Subjugated Macedonians Ask Independent State, Detroit Free Press (Detroit, Michigan), Oct 7, 1934, Page 133

[104] Assassin of King Receives Tribute, Detroit Free Press (Detroit, Michigan), Aug 31, 1936, Page 4

[105] I.K. Bezoff, Macedonian Says Greece is Hardest on His People, Detroit Free Press (Detroit, Michigan), Nov 14, 1937, Page 7

[106] Gregory Michaelidis, Salvation Abroad: Macedonian Migration to North America and the Making of Modern Macedonia, 1870-1970, University of Maryland Ph.D. Dissertation, 2005, Pg. 153,154.

[107] Protest to Bulgaria, The Indianapolis Star (Indianapolis, Indiana), May 23, 1938, Page 18

[108] Balkan Peace Effort Urged, Poughkeepsie Eagle-News (Poughkeepsie, New York), Sep 7, 1938, Page 12

[109] Alfred Tyrnauer, Nazi's Deadlies Led by Assassin Queen, World's News, Sydney, Nov. 29, 1941. Pg. 2.

[110] Bulgarian Talent to Present Play, The Akron Beacon Journal (Akron, Ohio), Dec 30, 1926, Page 19

[111] Walter Blondyn, Macedonians Condemn Axis Hold On Balkans, The Akron Beacon Journal (Akron, Ohio) 17 Aug 1941, Page 30

[112] Oscar Smith, Macedonians Turn Eyes to Homeland,   The Akron Beacon Journal (Akron, Ohio) 28 Jun 1938, Page 11

[113] Macedonian-Americans to Grame Plea for Postwar Liberation of Native Land, The Akron Beacon Journal (Akron, Ohio), Feb 27, 1944, Page 40

[114] Walter Blondyn, Creation of Macedonian Independent State After War Aked of FDR, The Akron Beacon Journal (Akron, Ohio), Jun 18, 1944, Page 44

[115] Jeanne May, Cyril Johns: Embraced American Life, Freedom,   Detroit Free Press (Detroit, Michigan) 27 Mar 2002, Page 71

[116] Luben Dimitroff, Peace in the Balkans, The Indianapolis News (Indianapolis, Indiana), Sep 19, 1945, Page 10

[117] Course Seen Only Ease For Balkan Unrest, The Indianapolis Star (Indianapolis, Indiana), Aug 31, 1947, Page 15

[118] Christ Anastasoff, A Balkan Switzerland, The Courier-Journal (Louisville, Kentucky), Sep 7, 1949, Page 6

[119] Macedonians Declare Stand, The Ottawa Citizen (Ottawa, Ontario, Canada), Aug 20, 1952, Page 10

[120] Hoosier Macedonians Issue Alert, The Indianapolis Star (Indianapolis, Indiana), Oct 14, 1956, Page 55

[121] Carrying The Torch for Freedom, The Indianapolis Star (Indianapolis, Indiana), Jul 1, 1956, Page 112

[122] Macedonians Set Day of Mourning, The Indianapolis Star (Indianapolis, Indiana), Oct 11, 1958, Page 3

[123] Macedonians Here Mourn Tito's Yoke, Alton Evening Telegraph (Alton, Illinois), Oct 11, 1958, Page 1

[124] Freedom Fighters All, The Indianapolis News (Indianapolis, Indiana), Oct 12, 1962 · Main Edition, Page 10

[125] Group Protests Visit by Tito, The Pittsburgh Press (Pittsburgh, Pennsylvania), Oct 11, 1963, Page 5

[126] American Macedonians Seek Halt of US Aid to Tito, The Cincinnati Enquirer (Cincinnati, Ohio), Oct 11, 1964, Page 59

[127] Hristo Kostov, Contested Ethnic Identity: The Case of Macedonian Canadians in Toronto, 1940-1996, Ph.D. Thesis, Department of History, University of Ottawa, 2009, Pg. 199.

[128] Riot in Church on Iron Curtin Politics, Chicago Tribune (Chicago, Illinois), Apr 6, 1948, Page 5

[129] Announce Parade for Macedonian Clubs on Monday, Harrisburg Telegraph (Harrisburg, Pennsylvania), Sep 4, 1926, Page 9

[130] Riot in Church on Iron Curtin Politics, Chicago Tribune (Chicago, Illinois), Apr 6, 1948, Page 5

[131] See Victor Sinadinoski, David Nakoff: Leader of Steelton's Macedonians and Founder of the First Macedonian-American Orthodox Church, 2018.

[132] Commonwealth V. Minoff, https://www.leagle.com/decision/1949650363pa2871607 . Accessed October 13, 2018.

[133] Indiana Annual Non-Profit Corporation Report: The Macedonian Political Organization of the United States of America and Canada, Indiana Secretary of State, January 10, 1944

[134] Indiana Annual Non-Profit Corporation Report: The Macedonian Political Organization of the United States of America and Canada, Indiana Secretary of State, February 7, 1951

[135] Indiana Annual Non-Profit Corporation Report: The Macedonian Political Organization of the United States of America and Canada, Indiana Secretary of State, January 17, 1952

[136] Indiana Annual Non-Profit Corporation Report: The Macedonian Political Organization of the United States of America and Canada, Indiana Secretary of State, January 19, 1953

[137] Indiana Annual Non-Profit Corporation Report: The Macedonian Political Organization of the United States of America and Canada, Indiana Secretary of State, January 22, 1954

[138] Indiana Annual Non-Profit Corporation Report: The Macedonian Political Organization of the United States of America and Canada, Indiana Secretary of State, January 14, 1955

[139] Indiana Annual Non-Profit Corporation Report: The Macedonian Patriotic Organization of the United States of America and Canada, Indiana Secretary of State, January 24, 1957

[140] Indiana Annual Non-Profit Corporation Report: The Macedonian Patriotic Organization of the United States of America and Canada, Indiana Secretary of State, January 14, 1960

[141] Indiana Annual Non-Profit Corporation Report: The Macedonian Patriotic Organization of the United States of America and Canada, Indiana Secretary of State, February 3, 1967

[142] Hristo Kostov, Contested Ethnic Identity: The Case of Macedonian Canadians in Toronto, 1940-1996, Ph.D. Thesis, Department of History, University of Ottawa, 2009, Pg. 170.

[143] Hristo Kostov, Contested Ethnic Identity: The Case of Macedonian Canadians in Toronto, 1940-1996, Ph.D. Thesis, Department of History, University of Ottawa, 2009, Pg. 202-203.

[144] Hristo Kostov, Contested Ethnic Identity: The Case of Macedonian Canadians in Toronto, 1940-1996, Ph.D. Thesis, Department of History, University of Ottawa, 2009, Pg. 203.

[145] Indiana Annual Non-Profit Corporation Report: The Macedonian Patriotic Organization of the United States of America and Canada, Indiana Secretary of State, February 3, 1967

[146] Hristo Kostov, Contested Ethnic Identity: The Case of Macedonian Canadians in Toronto, 1940-1996, Ph.D. Thesis, Department of History, University of Ottawa, 2009, Pg. 201.

[147] Virginia Nizamoff, Surso, https://web.archive.org/web/19971014012707/http://www.macedonian.org:80/ . Last accessed October 11, 2018.

[148] Indiana Annual Non-Profit Corporation Report: The Macedonian Patriotic Organization of the United States of America and Canada, Indiana Secretary of State, February 27, 1974; February 27, 1978; January 12, 1976; March 27, 1979; August 30, 1980.

[149] Indiana Annual Non-Profit Corporation Report: The Macedonian Patriotic Organization of the United States of America and Canada, Indiana Secretary of State, November 4, 1983

[150] Macedonian Tribune Past Editors, http://macedonian.org/joomla/index.php?option=com_content&view=article&id=52&Itemid=62 . Last accessed October 4, 2018.

[151] MPO Circular Letter by Ivan A Lebamoff and Dita Atzeff to all officers and members of the local chapters of the MPO, September 6, 1990.

[152] Radko is Gone: Several Compatriots Share Their Feelings About the Death of Ivano Miahiloff, September 1990.

[153] Macedonia, A Free State, The Indianapolis News (Indianapolis, Indiana), Mar 27, 1992 · Main Edition, Page 12

[154] Macedonia Republic Seeks Recognition, The Indianapolis News (Indianapolis, Indiana), May 29, 1992 · Main Edition, Page 9

[155] On Macedonia, The Indianapolis Star (Indianapolis, Indiana), Dec 31, 1993, Page 10

[156] https://groups.google.com/forum/#!topic/alt.news.macedonia/fJcwKeGQt3M . Last accessed October 11, 2018.

[157] A Basis for U.S. Support for the Republic of Macedonia, Macedonian Tribune, June 2001

[158]

https://web.archive.org/web/20021127212211/http://www.macedonian.org:80 / . Last accessed October 11, 2018.

[159] Letter from MPO President Chris Evanoff to President George W. Bush, March 9, 2004

[160]

https://web.archive.org/web/19971014012707/http://www.macedonian.org:80 / . Last accessed October 11, 2018.

[161] George Lebamoff, An American Macedonian, http://www.promacedonia.org/en/gl/index.html . Last Accessed October 11, 2018.

[162] Matjaz Klemenicic, The Reactions of Immigrants from the South Slavic Lands and their Descendants in the USA to the Dissolution of Yugoslavia (1989-1993), Pg. 45.

[163] Lubomir Todorov, MPO: 90 Years of Struggle for a Macedonian State, A Keynote speech delivered at the Grand Banquet of the 91st Annual MPO Convention in Fort Wayne, Indiana, September 2, 2012.

[164] Hristo Kostov, Contested Ethnic Identity: The Case of Macedonian Canadians in Toronto, 1940-1996, Ph.D. Thesis, Department of History, University of Ottawa, 2009, Pg. 285.

[165] Hristo Kostov, Contested Ethnic Identity: The Case of Macedonian Canadians in Toronto, 1940-1996, Ph.D. Thesis, Department of History, University of Ottawa, 2009, Pg. 204-205.

[166] Hristo Kostov, Contested Ethnic Identity: The Case of Macedonian Canadians in Toronto, 1940-1996, Ph.D. Thesis, Department of History, University of Ottawa, 2009, Pg. 203.

[167] https://groups.google.com/forum/#!topic/alt.news.macedonia/fJcwKeGQt3M . Last accessed October 11, 2018.

[168] https://groups.google.com/forum/#!topic/alt.news.macedonia/fJcwKeGQt3M . Last accessed October 11, 2018.

[169] Hristo Kostov, Contested Ethnic Identity: The Case of Macedonian Canadians in Toronto, 1940-1996, Ph.D. Thesis, Department of History, University of Ottawa, 2009, Pg. 304.

[170] Lubomir Todorov, MPO: 90 Years of Struggle for a Macedonian State, A Keynote speech delivered at the Grand Banquet of the 91st Annual MPO Convention in Fort Wayne, Indiana, September 2, 2012.

[171] https://groups.google.com/forum/#!topic/alt.news.macedonia/fJcwKeGQt3M . Last accessed October 11, 2018.

[172] Macedonian Ambassador Greets Banquet Attendants, Macedonian Tribune, Vol. 82, No. 3379

[173] Macedonian Ambassador Urges Macedonians to Look Forward, 2002 MPO Convention Address

[174] Bulgarian Ambassador Speaks to Delegates, 81st Annual MPO Convention, September 2002

[175] Letter from MPO President Chris Evanoff to Spas Tashev, September 28, 1998.

[176] https://groups.google.com/forum/#!topic/alt.news.macedonia/fJcwKeGQt3M . Last accessed October 11, 2018.

[177] Hristo Kostov, Contested Ethnic Identity: The Case of Macedonian Canadians in Toronto, 1940-1996, Ph.D. Thesis, Department of History, University of Ottawa, 2009, Pg. 204.

[178] Letter from MPO President Chris Evanoff to Ljupco Zikov, 2005, https://forums.vmacedonia.com/archive/index.php/t-18239.html . Last accessed October 4, 2018.

[179] https://web.archive.org/web/20061223105205/http://www.macedonian.org:80 / . Last accessed October 11, 2018.

[180] A Message from MPO Advisor Larry Koroloff, Macedonian Tribune, 2010. (Unknown month).

[181] Dusan Sinadinoski, АНТИМАКЕДОНЦИ ЌЕ ГИ ПОПИШУВААТ МАКЕДОНЦИТЕ, January 26, 2010. http://www.globusmagazin.com.mk/default-mk.asp?ItemID=F87484DBCC63B74384CA07783CB1A583&arc=1 . Last accessed October 13, 2018.

[182] UMD Removes MPO from Census Project Coalition, February 23, 2010, http://macedoniaonline.eu/content/view/12671/1/ . Accessed October 13, 2018.

[183] Fred Meacnhoff, A Message from MPO Treasurer Fred Meacnhoff, Macedonian Tribune, May 5, 2011, Page 4.

[184] Македонска Патриотична Организација- 91ви конгрес в САЩ, Published by Muzuna-BG on September 10, 2012, https://www.youtube.com/watch?v=EkP4IkrwEFA&feature=plcp .

[185] Lubomir Todorov, MPO: 90 Years of Struggle for a Macedonian State, A Keynote speech delivered at the Grand Banquet of the 91st Annual MPO Convention in Fort Wayne, Indiana, September 2, 2012.

[186] United Macedonian Diaspora Advisory Council, http://umdiaspora.org/cpt_team_group/umd-advisory-council/page/2/ . Last Accessed October 14, 2018.

[187]

https://groups.yahoo.com/neo/groups/MacedonianMediaMonitor/conversations/topics/3908 . Accessed October 13, 2018.

[188] [188]

https://groups.yahoo.com/neo/groups/MacedonianMediaMonitor/conversations/topics/3908 . Accessed October 13, 2018.

[189]

https://groups.yahoo.com/neo/groups/MacedonianMediaMonitor/conversations/topics/3908 . Last accessed October 13, 2018.